Room for

Change your home & enhance your life with tools, tips & inspirational DIY projects

Improvement

BARBARA K, DIY diva

RODALE

This edition first published in the UK in 2005 by
Rodale International Ltd
7–10 Chandos Street
London W1G 9AD
www.rodalebooks.co.uk

A CIP record for this book is available from the British Library
ISBN 1-4050-8801-X

Printed and bound in China using acid-free paper

Book design by Ellen Nygaard and Emma Ashby

Illustrations by Nick Higgins
Interior photographs by Lewis Bloom and George Ross
Cover photograph by Arthur Elgort; makeup by Sonia Kashuk; hair by Maria Barca

1 3 5 7 9 8 6 4 2

This paperback edition distributed to the book trade by Pan Macmillan Ltd

Notice
The writers and editors who compiled this book have tried to make all the contents as accurate and correct as possible. Photographs and text have been carefully checked and cross-checked. However, due to the variability of personal skill, tools, materials, and so on, neither the writers nor Rodale International Ltd assume any responsibility for any injuries suffered or for damages or other losses that result from the material presented herein. All instructions should be carefully studied and clearly understood before embarking on any project.

   Mention of specific companies, organizations, or authorities in this book does not imply endorsement by the publisher, nor does mention of specific companies, organizations, or authorities imply that they endorse this book.

   Internet addresses and telephone numbers given in this book were accurate at the time it went to press.

RODALE
LIVE YOUR WHOLE LIFE™

We inspire and enable people to improve their lives and the world around them

To my dad. Thank you, Dad, for all your support, love and

patience throughout the years, and for all the building projects and blocks

you gave me. I love you more than words can say.

To my mom for encouraging me to keep swimming on all those

cold days and for her support, love and patience. Mom, you were my

first role model for an independent woman and I love you!

And to Zachary Kavovit-Murphy – my beautiful son and newest inspiration.

You are the absolute love and light of my life.

Contents

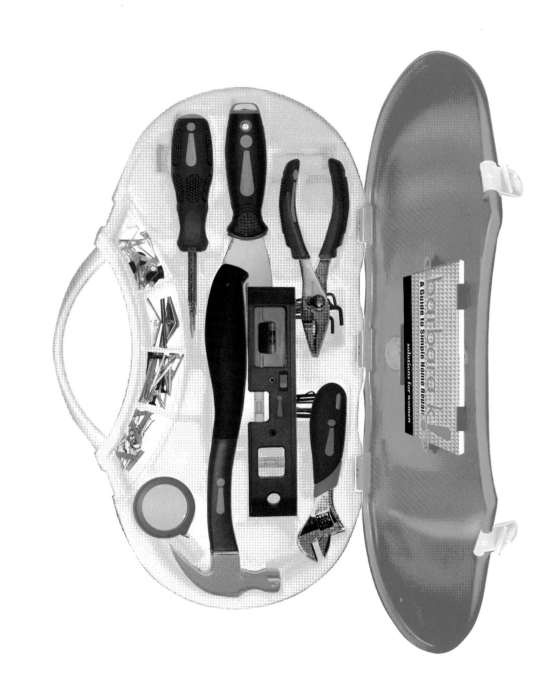

Acknowledgements

First, I would like to thank my mom and dad for giving me love and support throughout my life. Thank you also to my awesome sister, Caryn, for always being there for me over the years.

Special thanks to Sam Gradess – you were not only one of my very first investors but also someone who encouraged me with your wise counsel, which enabled me to have greater clarity over the years. Your endless and tireless support, total understanding and commitment to the barbara k! brand and to me helped get me through periods of uncertainty. Thank you so very much for your personal encouragement when it mattered the most; you are a true friend.

I would also like to thank the following people for their endless hours and effort in making this book possible:

Mel Berger, my literary agent at the William Morris Agency: Mel, thank you for believing in the brand, this book and me.

Margot Schupf, my editor at Rodale: Wow! Now I know you are the best editor in the world. Thanks for all your focus, awesome commitment, believing in me and seeing this project through.

Ellen Nygaard, book designer, thanks for all your creativity. To everyone else at Rodale: Thank you for all your hard work, creativity and dedication.

Karen Kelly: A special thanks to you for doing such a great job capturing my voice and organizing my thoughts on paper. You brought things out of me that I don't think anyone else could have.

Lewis Bloom and George Ross, the photographers: You both made me look and feel great.

Michelle Bergerson at Cityscape Design: Thank you for your beautiful designs, commitment and energy in making this book a success.

barbara k! Thanks

Rome was not built in a day and neither was barbara k! It takes a small army and many dedicated people to build a brand. I have been very fortunate to attract 'entrepreneurs' in their own right who have assisted me in reaching my goals. They are a group of optimistic people who focus on solutions, not problems. Everyone at barbara k! over the past two years has been loyal, patient and dedicated. These are wonderful people whom I respect and admire and who have appreciated my vision to go the distance and be team players. To them I owe enormous thanks.

Additional Thanks

There are a few people in my professional life that I have to single out and thank as they have been with me throughout most of my entrepreneurial years stemming from my construction days.

BJ Toner: You have been with me since very early on in my business life and youth. Thanks for being a person I can rely on and trust and for keeping me organized in some of my more insane moments! Your loyalty will always be appreciated, and thanks for sticking by me through all the good times and not so good times!

Takeesha Banks: 'My Keesha Girl'. You are a shining star! You have been there every hour, every minute, every day. You are so much more than my assistant but a stable support for me. You are my 'sister' and friend. Simply put, I could not have had my personal and professional life so completely organized. Thanks for your endless love and support of me. You are a true role model for the independent woman!

Kurt Straub: You have been working with me since the construction days and I am thrilled we are still together! Thanks for all your endless days on the photo shoots making sure all the projects came off without a hitch. Your loyalty and commitment are so appreciated throughout so many years in the construction days.

Kevin Glaser: Seems like only yesterday when we first met on the slopes and suddenly I had a company with more than one person. Thanks for all your past commitment and dedication to the brand and to me. I will never forget our first trip to Taiwan, all the fun we've had, and where we came from. You will always be considered an integral part of barbara k!

Still More Thanks

Brad Rose: It's not often that you meet an attorney who becomes instrumental in helping you reach your goals and has the same sense of urgency you do. Thank you for all your guidance and thanks to Pryor Cashman Sherman Flynn for believing in me and going the distance.

TestRite International: Special thanks to Judy Lee and the entire TestRite staff for their belief in me at such an early stage. Thanks for your patience and guidance and for making superior quality products.

John Lonczak: Thank you for your knowledge and expertise in product design.

Thanks to all the retailers who took a chance on an unknown named Barbara K, particularly Charlie Chinni and JCPenney, for giving us our first chance at retail.

Bill and Sheila McCaffery from McCaffery Ratner Gottlieb & Lane: Thanks for nurturing me through my first advertising campaign.

To my investors: Thank you very much for believing in me and supporting me throughout the growth of barbara k!

Zeny and Fernando: Thanks for keeping me on time and organized.

Maria Barca: Thanks for always making sure I shine!

Finally, special thanks to my loyal customers who have helped me make my dreams a reality.

Introduction

My Story

Here I am about to inspire you to take control of the home around you and make your dream house a reality. A lot of people who knew me 'way back when' may think I am the most unlikely person to do that, based on my academic track record. My school teachers would say to my parents, 'She's a smart girl … but she can't seem to focus.' Of course I couldn't – I was already dreaming up my first business!

I am the founder of a brand and lifestyle company, for women, called barbara k! But I'm also the girl next door listening to rock and roll at a party, whom you said hello to on the beach or spotted shopping at the supermarket. I'm a happy-go-lucky ordinary kid who had no more opportunity than anybody else, but who turned an idea into a Big Business. Do you recognize yourself in my description? Most likely, you do.

Some people say I've been lucky. If being lucky means recognizing and then seizing an opportunity, then, yes, I'm the luckiest person in the world. The first ingredient to fulfilling your personal dreams and becoming a successful entrepreneur is being aware of the possibilities around you every day. The second is acknowledging and appreciating what you're good at and turning it into the basis of something great. For me, it was a childhood skill with Lego.

Accomplishment and self-esteem go hand in hand. That's where *Room for Improvement* comes in. This book will show you how easy it is to use tools around the house, which will enable you to improve your environment. And that will help give you the independence you need to take charge of your life. Facing big issues such as job loss, divorce, financial problems or just day-to-day challenges will be easier once you have gained the confidence and self-reliance that comes from self-sufficiency. I know it's true – I've seen it happen in my own life and in other women's lives.

This conviction comes from every experience I've had. I was a dreamer as a child – a cockeyed optimist, in fact. I still am. I was raised in the Bronx, which taught me some hard-core life lessons. If you wanted something – anything – there was probably going to be a fight for it. Ensuring the neighbourhood bullies didn't push me off my bike was part of everyday life. That and the fact that there was so much emphasis placed on academics by my mother, a history teacher and later an assistant head teacher of a tough school, helped mould my character.

My dad also had a hand in my future. He was good at building things, and he always included me in his projects. Once he built my sister, Caryn, and me a bunk bed. He would point to a part of it and say, 'Barbara, Caryn – nail this.' We would take turns with his hammer and bang away. The awkward feeling of the outsized, heavy hammer in my hand was dwarfed in comparison to the great sense of accomplishment I felt when I was finished. It's a feeling I remember and cherish to this day.

Learning to swim also taught me to push for my dreams, even when faced with hardship. My mother would take Caryn and me to swimming lessons in Montauk, New York. The lessons were held early in the summer season, but no matter how cold or rainy it was, my mother would be out there with us making sure we went through our strokes. This taught me persistence, and physical and emotional strength. Nothing is easy, and that goes for swimming in a chilly ocean, but you have to keep going if you want to achieve anything. So today, when things get a little challenging at work, I tell my staff to 'keep swimming'.

After college, I tried my hand on Wall Street, but it wasn't for me. At the same time, in 1989, there was a construction boom in New York. My mother and her friends complained about contractors and repairmen who didn't show up. A lightbulb went off over my head. I thought, 'I can do something about this. What about a woman helping women get projects done around the house?'

I had the local stationers make up flyers and business cards. I named the business Stand-Ins. I put my brochures through every door within a 16-km radius of my house, and I'd stand outside upmarket shopping centres in my area and introduce myself to every woman and give her my card. I would say, 'I'm Barbara and I can help you fix anything in your house.' No job was too small or too big: I'd clean and fix anything – repair cracked tiles, clean gutters and change doorknobs.

My instincts were right: I got a lot of calls. Suddenly, I had jobs but no real home repair experience. So I got a copy of the local phone book and called every handyman listed. I told them I would find and take them to jobs (often because I wanted to make sure they showed up) and bring them home again. I supervised their work and made sure every job got done. I learned home repair, communication skills and plain old-fashioned market research simply by diving in and learning by doing. I was eager to put on a tool belt with a hammer and tape measure hanging from it. I thought it was a really cool and sexy look.

After the business took off, I wrote a letter to the head buyer for the IBM headquarters located near my home. I told him Stand-Ins could assist in any repairs at a moment's notice. I followed up with a phone call but had no luck. Did it stop me? No. After an unrelenting campaign of calls and letters, I wore him down and was invited in for a meeting. He asked me point blank, 'What can you do for IBM?' I said, 'I can repair and improve your offices with a moment's notice. Anything you need fixed, I can fix.' The result was a 2-year small repair contract at the IBM corporate headquarters.

Things started happening very quickly after that. For example, a business associate told me about a developer who was looking for women contractors. There were advantages to hiring women and minorities, especially when the developer had union problems (like this one did). I didn't know anything much about unions, but when I met with the developer, he told me I would have to negotiate with its leaders. I gave it my best shot and was awarded a lucrative contract. By 1993 I had been in business for two years. I bought a van, leased an office and hired a couple of carpenters and project managers. It was difficult since I was in a tough, male-dominated industry. And I got bruises – men called me names and threatened me. It was just like growing up in the Bronx. I took it in my stride. When you're on to something, it's to be expected.

Eventually I decided to take a chance on the construction business. I formed a new company, Anchor Construction, which focused on corporate and commercial construction. I was finally breaking through the 'glass ceiling'. Anchor landed construction projects for high-profile corporations such as Bloomingdales, Carnegie Hall and others. These companies liked the fact that Anchor was woman-owned and -operated. They counted on me to always do my best on a job … even though there may have been problems during the course of that job.

During this time, I met my former husband, who was an inspiration to me in the rough-and-tumble construction world. And we had our son, Zachary. By 2000 I was doing millions of dollars' worth of business and earned a name in the industry. I was even cited as being one of the '100 Most Influential Women in Business in New York City'.

Despite these successes, I kept thinking about the women from my early days. Why did they have to rely on no-show contractors, husbands, brothers, fathers or neighbours? Generations of women have been fearful of anything going wrong in their home – yet few of them have the knowledge or skills to do anything about it. Feeling comfortable about doing home improvement was the 'final frontier' for women. I saw an opportunity to 'change the gene pool' and recreate the way women felt about using tools. That meant convincing women that tools could change their life and that they were just accessories like their shoes, belts, bags and emery boards. They simply could not survive without them!

I knew women would respond to great-looking products that also worked and were made just for them. A hammer is so big and ugly – why can't it look and feel good in your hand? Why couldn't I recreate what women have come to expect to see from tools without changing their function? Wouldn't tools like that appeal to women's practical and creative sides? It's important for women to realize the many applications for tools. For example, how good would it feel to say, 'Yes, I can help you with that' when your children ask you to raise a bicycle seat or fix a toy?

Then, almost simultaneously, 9/11 happened and the construction business, my marriage, as well as life itself seemed to collapse. One evening during that difficult time, I was watching *Sex and the City*. The character Samantha was trying unsuccessfully to hang a curtain; she had to call her boyfriend who would not come over and help her. I thought, 'This is a totally modern, independent woman, and she can't put up a curtain rod!' And it all clicked into place. I knew I was right. If she had the perfect, stylish tool kit, she could do it herself.

That idea prompted me to call a prototype maker. He asked me if I had an engineered drawing of the tool kit case that I had in mind. I didn't, so I went on a quest and found someone to make a CAD drawing. Finally, my idea was translated into one beautiful kidney-shaped tool case. A 'star' (my tool case) was born.

After intense research, I located a manufacturer and a sourcing company called TestRite, in Taiwan. In no time, I was sitting in their boardroom. The president of the company was a woman, and even though we came from two very different cultures, she immediately understood what I was trying to accomplish. She took one look at the tool kit and said, 'This is the best idea I have ever seen.' Right then and there, she committed to making the moulds for a set of tools based on the original tool case design. The company was instrumental in getting the product side of my business off the ground.

Ultimately barbara k! and *Room for Improvement* are about self-determination and independence. Tools are simply one way of helping you get there. It's not about perfection. It's not about being 'tool girl' and walking around with a power saw. It's about stepping-stones. It's about making mistakes, learning from them and getting it right the next time. 'Fix my running toilet' – done! 'Hang my picture' – done! 'Tell him "I have had enough" ' – done! 'Get that new job' – done!

Life changes like the ocean – so fast! It takes a great set of tools to get you through it. Becoming a self-sufficient, independent woman is probably the greatest gift I gave myself. I hope that *Room for Improvement* inspires you to fearlessly enhance your home and go after your dreams so that you too can take charge of your life.

Keep on swimming!

Barbara K

Tools Rule

Every tool is a 'power tool' in my opinion. That's because, when used properly, the right tool can help you fix a broken doorknob, un-squeak a squeaky door or help hang meaningful photographs and mementos on the walls of your home. The result? You'll start your day off on the right foot because you won't be battling a flimsy doorknob or a faulty lock, you'll no longer be annoyed by the noisy door and you'll be surrounded by beautiful things that you love. And it all starts when you pick up a hammer!

I truly believe that tools can change your life. Sure, you can call a handyman (and most likely it will be a man), and he can replace some rotting moulding around your door. You can hire a plumber to rid your sink of a nasty blockage or replace some ancient bathroom fixtures. You can pay some teenagers to paint your living room. You can wait forever for someone else in your household (names will not be mentioned!) to get off the couch and fix it (whatever it is) for you. Or you can make your dream home a reality yourself!

Why wait? Knowing how to do your own simple home repairs and decorating and design jobs gives you control over your own life and home. Wouldn't it be liberating not to have to depend on the skills and the empty promises of a stranger when it comes to your home? And even if you choose to hire people to perform certain repair jobs, wouldn't it be great to know whether or not they are doing the jobs properly and you're getting your money's worth?

So let's start at the beginning, with the tools of your new trade.

How to Select Tools

Having the right tools will help you perform both simple tasks and more complex jobs with ease and security. Shoddy tools or those that are wrong for a particular job may break; worse, they can cause you to hurt yourself if you're not able to use them properly. But high-quality tools, carefully chosen and appropriate for both you and the job at hand, will make your life easier while adding enjoyment to your design and decorating jobs. The right tools, used according to the manufacturers' instructions, are paramount to your safety, performance and success.

So how do you select the right tools? Once you've decided what you need (we'll talk about which tools in detail in 'Barbara K's Basic Tool Kit' on page 41), go to the DIY store and handle the tools. Are all the edges smooth? Do the tools feel good in your hand? Do the power tools come with warranties? There is no reason why a set of tools shouldn't last a long time and be passed on to the next generation. Wouldn't you love to know

ARE YOU A BAG OR BOX WOMAN?

Once you have your tools assembled, you should keep them somewhere close at hand so that you can grab them quickly when a doorknob comes loose or a hole needs patching. Should you invest in a snappy metal or heavy-duty plastic toolbox or should you choose a snazzy and soft canvas or leather tool bag? Either way, you should be proud to show off your tools and their carrying case. Personally, I prefer to keep my tools in my hard, slim blue plastic case that slips easily into a kitchen drawer and looks great when I pull it out (or displayed on the worktop). But, of course, there are pros and cons to both options, as I explain here.

Some women feel that a toolbox, with its rigid sides and layers of storage, is excellent for keeping smaller bits and pieces organized. But other women I know say that metal boxes can rust, and metal toolboxes can scratch floors when moved around. One way to alleviate this problem is by sticking soft circular pads to the bottom of the box. (These adhesive circular pads are often used on the bottom of chair legs and other furniture to prevent floors from being marked or scratched.)

A sturdy canvas or leather bag won't mark your floor or rust. But unless it has lots of pockets for smaller tools, such as a nail set or a compass and tiny

bits like nails and screws, these items may fall to the bottom of the bag and become nearly impossible to find. But if you do choose the bag option, you will have a lot of choices. Canvas bags come in all shapes and sizes, and you don't necessarily have to buy one in a DIY store. You can express your style by using a colourful beach bag or a canvas tote found at your favourite boutique.

Finally, if you're going to store your tools outside in a garage or shed, a plastic box will be less susceptible to rust than a metal one. If you plan on keeping your tools inside your house in an understairs cupboard or even a drawer, a bag could be a better option for you.

that your daughter or son will someday use the same tools you so proudly put to work in making their childhood home a great place to live?

Setting Up a Workspace

No matter where you put your workspace, take the time to personalize the area and make it your own. There's no law that says a work area has to be grim and grey. In fact, it should be a happy, fun area – one you look forward to using! Consider painting work surfaces in your favourite colour. A brown worktable is boring; a lavender one isn't! If your workspace does double duty in the kitchen or utility room, don't despair. You can find a small tarpauline (for protecting surfaces) in many colours. And canvas dust sheets can be painted or dyed to suit your fancy. If you take the time to personalize your space and make it attractive, you'll be more prone to use it.

Here are some practical considerations to bear in mind when setting up a workspace of your own.

• Make sure your space is well lit. Being able to see what you are doing is of paramount importance for the sake of both safety and accuracy.

• If you are working at a table that is used for something else (such as food preparation or after-school homework), make sure you have a cover to place over the table when working. This protects the surface, of course, and also makes cleaning up easier: you can simply gather up your cover and slide any waste into the bin.

• Put a wet-and-dry vacuum cleaner on the top of your to-buy list; they're relatively inexpensive and will make wet or dry cleaning up easy. And you won't have to worry about destroying that expensive vacuum cleaner that you use around your home.

• Have a wide-mouthed waste bin nearby. Cleaning up will be easy, especially if you line it with contractor's grade bags. They are tough and virtually impossible to tear. The good news is you can find them in any DIY store.

• An easily accessible power source is a must. The cords on power tools are usually quite short. So a tough 2–3 metre extension reel will allow you to move around easily and safely with your power drill or sander.

• If your workspace is in a garage or shed, some kind of heat source, such as a space heater, will come in handy when the autumn winds begin to blow and temperatures are cooler.

We've Got You Pegged!

MAKE A PEG-BOARD TOOL STORAGE RACK
Time: About 3 hours

Setting up a tool and material storage area on the back of a cupboard door, in a spare bedroom or even in your garage is a simple, inexpensive process. Peg-Board is a great material that can be cut to any size and painted any colour under the sun. Its small holes hold a variety of metal hooks and holders especially designed to hold tools and other objects securely.

Peg-Board racks can hold more than tools: craft supplies, beauty supplies, children's toys and kitchen equipment can find a home on this simple hanging system.

WHAT YOU NEED
Tape measure
Peg-Board, cut to desired size
50 × 25-mm (2 × 1-in) planed softwood battens
Stud finder
12 50-mm (2-in) wood screws
Anchors (if not screwing Peg-Board into studs)
Power drill with twist drill, masonry drill and screwdriver bits
Safety glasses
Mitre box and saw
12 19-mm (¾-in) wood screws for Peg-Board
Assorted Peg-Board hooks and holders, depending on your needs

HOW TO GET IT DONE
1. To make the rack, first measure the wall where you will install your rack with a tape measure. Position the rack according to your height. You shouldn't have to reach uncomfortably to get at the top-most items on the board.
2. Once you have determined the height and width of the space available, take your measurement to the DIY store and have them cut the Peg-Board to size. You may have to buy an entire sheet, which often comes in 2440 × 1220-mm (8 × 4-ft) sheets. The remaining pieces can be used for

another board somewhere else in the house – in the kitchen, office or inside a cupboard door. While you are at the DIY store, pick up a length of 50 × 25-mm (2 × 1-in) planed softwood batten, enough to frame the inside perimeter of the cut Peg-Board.

3. If you are screwing the frame into partition wall, find the wooden studs in the wall with a stud finder. Studs are typically located every 400 mm (16 in) from the centre of the wall. Screwing into studs is the most secure way to hang a rack that will hold heavy tools. If the place where you have chosen to install your rack does not match up with the wall studs, you will also have to use cavity anchors to hold the screws in place.

   If you are screwing the frame into masonry, such as a concrete garage wall, you will need to use masonry drill bits and wall plugs. (See 'Screwing into Partition and Masonry Walls' on page 24 for specific instructions on using screws and anchors.)

4. Put on safety glasses. Cut the battens to fit around the outside edge of the Peg-Board with a mitre box and saw. Create a frame and screw it into the wall where the Peg-Board will go. Use 50-mm (2-in) screws if you are screwing into wall studs or masonry screws if you're screwing it into masonry. Screw all four corners of the frame into place and then screw it in two equidistant places on all four sides. There is no need to attach the pieces to each other before they go on the wall. Create the frame as you attach each piece to the wall. This installation method allows the Peg-Board to float off the wall, making room for the hooks to fit properly in the holes. Fix the strips with their wider face flat to the wall.

5. Once the frame is installed, you can screw the Peg-Board to the frame using the 19-mm (¾-in) wood screws. Be sure to screw all four corners and then screw it in two equidistant places on all four sides. Avoid those spots where the frame is screwed into the wall.

6. Add the Peg-Board hooks and holders, and simply hang up your tools and supplies.

SCREWING INTO PARTITION AND MASONRY WALLS

With the right bits, screws and anchors you can drill into any wall in your house. If you're drilling into a partition wall, use a standard twist bit. If you're drilling into masonry or plaster, use a masonry bit. Similarly, use the right type of fixing for the surface you're working with: a wood screw for partition walls and a screw and wall plug for masonry or plaster walls.

As I mentioned in step 3 of the Peg-Board project, unless you can drive screws into wall studs, you need to install anchors in the wall before attaching the rack with screws. There are several different kinds of wall anchors, the two most common being wall plugs and cavity wall anchors. They can be made of plastic or metal.

A wall plug is used when going into solid material, such as concrete or masonry. The plug is installed by drilling a hole in the wall large enough to accommodate it snugly when tapped into the hole using a mallet or hammer covered with a rag to protect the surface of the wall. The plug expands in diameter as the screw is screwed into it.

The size of the hole you drill depends on the size of the wall plug. Furthermore, different sizes of plugs accommodate different size screws. Confused? Don't be. Choose plugs and screws according to the weight of the board and the tools it will be carrying. In the example of the Peg-Board tool storage rack, for example, if you are attaching the Peg-Board frame to masonry or plaster, use a wall plug that needs a 6.5-mm (¼-in) hole. That amount of holding power should be sufficient to carry a variety of power and hand tools. Here's how:

1. Put on safety glasses. Pre-drill holes in the object you want to hang.
2. Mark the wall through the pre-drilled holes in the object you want to hang so you can see where to drill the holes for the wall plugs. Then drill a hole using a masonry bit to fit the particular diameter and length of the plug. A masonry bit has a tungsten-carbide tip that allows it to cut through masonry. When drilling into a masonry wall, I recommend operating the power drill at a slow speed and backing it out frequently to pull out masonry debris and dust that will clog the hole and overheat the drill.
3. Insert the plug in the hole and tap it flush with the wall using a mallet or hammer covered with a rag to protect the surface of the wall. Repeat the process with the remaining plugs.
4. Insert standard screws of the appropriate size for the plugs into the holes and tighten. Hang the object.

A cavity wall anchor is used when attaching an item to partition walls. They are designed to spread out behind the partition and hold screws firmly in place.

In our Peg-Board example, if you are attaching the Peg-Board frame to a partition wall, use cavity wall anchors designed to hold up to 23 kg (50 lb) of weight each.

1. Put on safety glasses. Pre-drill holes in the object you want to hang, then mark the hole positions on the wall as described earlier.
2. Drill the holes using a standard twist bit to fit the particular diameter and length of the cavity wall anchor.
3. Insert the anchor in the hole and tap it flush with the wall using a mallet or hammer covered with a rag to protect the surface of the wall. Repeat the process with the remaining anchors.
4. Insert screws into the holes and tighten. Hang the object.

There's No Such Thing as Too Many Tools: A Glossary

It's frustrating to go to a DIY store only to be faced with aisles of gadgets, gizmos, instruments and implements and have no idea what they are or how they work. Right here, right now, I'll demystify the wild and wonderful world of tools. This glossary will enable you to go confidently to the store and ask for – and get – what you need!

GET A GRIP!

Bench vice

These are incredibly useful items to have: they can take the place of an AWOL teenager, a busy friend or a snoring spouse. And they don't talk back, either. Clamps steady things you are working on, or they secure glued items together while they dry.

A bench vice and a tabletop are all you need to hold an unwieldy piece of wood awaiting drilling or to act as a temporary vice on the edge of a workbench. Small spring clamps will hold veneer in place while glue is setting it permanently. They can even secure a canvas dust sheet to an outdoor worktable on a windy day. More specialized clamps perform other

exciting miracles of holding power! I personally recommend buying an inexpensive clamp-on bench vice with 100-mm (4-in) jaws. You can either temporarily attach this to a workbench or table and then store it away when it's not in use, or you can clamp it to a worktable and leave it there. Attach the vice to one end of your table instead of the middle of the table to leave yourself most of the table length to work.

C-clamp

Two 75-mm (3-in) C-clamps will handle almost any household project. A C-clamp holds work between a pad, which often swivels, and an anvil. Turning the spindle adjusts the grip. C-clamps are very inexpensive and also really versatile.

Corner clamp

This highly specialized clamp is perfect for holding mitred or picture frame corners together. It holds two pieces together at a 90-degree angle. Corner

clamps often feature a saw slot for cutting 45-degree angles.

Spring clamps

Spring clamps come in a variety of sizes and are made of either metal or plastic. They are perfect for holding thinner materials and useful for craft projects and small repair jobs. The plastic ones are not as sturdy as the metal ones. Either way, they're inexpensive, so it is worth having a set of them in various sizes.

Web clamp

Woodworkers mainly use web clamps to hold several wide pieces of wood that have been glued together. However, web clamps also have some application for anyone who is faced with a wobbly chair that needs re-gluing or a cabinet that needs to be held in place while each of its four sides are nailed together. This clamp is made up of a long and very sturdy nylon strap that can be wrapped around any item you are working on. A ratchet device tightens and holds the strap in place. Web clamps are expensive, though, so you can use a bungee cord to approximate the function of a web clamp.

Slip joint pliers

This gripping tool has two hinged arms and serrated jaws for better holding power. The movable joint allows the tool to adjust to two positions, one with a wider open position. Slip joint pliers can be used for a variety of holding tasks in woodworking, general repair and plumbing jobs – even craft projects. For example, you can get a stubborn nut off of a bolt more easily with slip joint pliers.

Adjustable spanner

The opening of this spanner adjusts by rotating a threaded adjuster with your thumb. What's great about an adjustable spanner is that you can change the size of the opening by millimetres, allowing you to hold or turn a variety of different-size objects. It's

especially useful if you are adjusting the height of a bicycle, for example. Adjustable spanners come in a wide variety of sizes. I recommend the 200-mm (8-in) or 300-mm (12-in) size for most household tasks, but they also come in 150-mm (6-in) and 250-mm (10-in) models.

Cable ties

Cable ties are lengths of sturdy plastic with an opening at the end that lets you slip the opposite end through it and pull it tight for a very strong grip. They come in a variety of lengths, according to their purpose, and lots of great colours. Cable ties can hold glued items together while the glue dries (you need to cut cable ties with a sturdy pair of scissors or snips). Cable ties are also great for tying up recycled newspapers and cardboard or for holding several computer or electronic wires together to keep them neat.

CUT IT UP

Utility knife

Utility knives are versatile because of their convenient size and retractable and replaceable extremely sharp blades. You can buy inexpensive plastic ones, but I recommend you get a good-

quality retractable utility knife. (It still won't be very expensive.) Always be sure to have extra blades on hand because you will want to change them often; a blunt blade is dangerous. For general cutting, use a standard single-edged reversible blade. When one side gets blunt, you can turn it around and use the other side. Just in case you get the urge to replace your kitchen floor, a scoring blade, which can be put into the same metal knife, can be used for cutting linoleum and vinyl.

Diagonal cutting pliers

These handy little clippers cut wire easily, and you may find them useful for other wire-cutting tasks as well. A standard 175-mm (7-in) model is the most versatile for doing simple electrical repairs.

Metal snips

Snips look like scissors with stubby blades. They are used for cutting sheet metal, but they also come in handy for

cutting chicken wire, screening, steel strapping and other metal items. Don't use metal snips to cut electrical wire: this type of wire can nick the blades and that may leave a ragged edge on your next cutting project.

Wood and cold chisels

There are many different kinds of wood chisels, but most household chiselling jobs can be accomplished with a basic set of four that will come in 6-, 12-, 19- and 25-mm (¼-, ½-, ¾- and 1-in) sizes. The better the quality of chisel set, the sharper and more precise the edge. You can use wood chisels to cut out a recess (often known as a mortise) for door hinges and other hardware. Cold chisels aren't as sharp as wood chisels

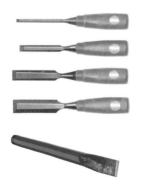

and are used on masonry. Always wear safety glasses when working with a cold chisel.

A BIT ABOUT DRILLS AND SCREWS

Allen or hex keys

The little screws with no heads that often come with flat pack assemble-it-yourself furniture are called 'setscrews'. You need an Allen key, sometimes known as a hex key, to put them in or remove them. Flat-pack furniture often comes with a small Allen key, but it's handy to have a set of Allen keys in your tool kit because chances are as

soon as you finish putting that TV stand together the Allen key that came with it will fall into a black hole never to return. When you want to disassemble any furniture that is put together with setscrews, you will have the necessary tool on hand. You can buy larger Allen keys individually if need be. They are very affordable.

Power and cordless drills

A power drill with variable speeds is truly a must-have in every home, especially if it reverses. A close cousin to the power drill is the cordless drill, which runs on rechargeable batteries.

Cordless drills have a tendency not to be as powerful as power drills, but they are certainly handy and don't encumber you with a flex. They do weigh more than power drills because the battery pack is at the base of the drill.

I developed a battery-powered drill that has a separate battery pack that is attached to the drill with a flexible cord. It hooks onto the waist of your trousers, making the drill itself lighter.

Your ability to get into tight spaces or do drilling jobs outside is enhanced with a cordless drill. You charge the battery pack by plugging it in overnight according to the manufacturer's instructions. Most power and cordless drills have a built-in tightening mechanism, making it easy to switch bit sizes and types.

Drill bits

You can buy drill bits in a variety of sizes, usually in convenient sets. Bits fit into both power and cordless drills and are standard in size, so you do not have to worry about matching brands. Twist bits are good for predrilling holes for screws and come in sizes to complement a whole range of screw sizes. Spade bits are good for drilling large holes. (For example, you'd use one of these bits to drill a larger hole in the back of a chest that you are converting into a television or stereo cabinet so that plugs and wires can easily fit through it.) Masonry bits drill into solid walls. They have tungsten-carbide tips that will not blunt when penetrating such hard material. Ceramic tile bits, which look like little spades, are perfect for drilling through glass and china. (You'd use this bit if you wanted to make a clock out of a pretty plate you found at a flea market. A ceramic tile bit will allow you to drill the proper hole through the middle so you can attach the clock works.)

Electric and cordless screwdrivers

An electric screwdriver can make driving screws easier than a manual screwdriver can, and it's lighter than a reversible drill. It makes light, simple work of basic screwing tasks.

Flat-tip screwdrivers

Flat-tip screwdrivers can sometimes be frustrating. Unless you match the size of the tip with the slot in the screw, it will easily slip out and end up 'stripping' the screw, which means that the soft metal of the screw will become nicked, widened and generally damaged and useless. So it's important to have a good set of flat-tip screwdrivers in a variety of sizes, from small to large.

You can also invest in a magnetic-tip ratchet screwdriver. The handle stays the same, and you can change heads or bits just as you would with a drill. These take up less room than a set of screwdrivers. But it is handy to have the variety of lengths a set of individual screwdrivers can offer – from the very tiny to the very large.

Phillips screwdrivers

A Phillips screwdriver has a little cross at the top of it, as does the screw itself. There is more flexibility in matching head to screw with a Phillips head because the cross allows the driver to grip the screw more tightly than does a flat-tip screwdriver.

6-in-1 screwdriver

A 6-in-1 screwdriver is a powerhouse of versatility and function. It offers two double-ended screwdriver bits, one double-ended nut/bolt driver, and one standard screwdriver grip/handle that provide the most commonly used sizes of flat-tip and Phillips-head screwdrivers as well as nut/bolt drivers in one handy tool.

WIRE WORK

Long nose pliers

These are useful for a variety of tasks. If you have ever made a beaded necklace or any kind of jewellery, for instance, you very well may have used long nose or finer needle nose pliers. A 175- or 200-mm (7- or 8-in) pair will allow you to form loops in wires or to get into tight spaces to grab the end of a wire (or other small items).

Mallet
A mallet looks like a large judge's gavel, only with a rubber head. They are lighter than standard metal hammers. Mallets are very useful for pounding objects you don't want to dent or break, such as the joints of wood furniture or a slab of flagstone. Mallets can be used to put forceful pressure behind anything that a metal hammer's head would damage because the concentrated force of a small hammer head is greater than the force of the larger surface of the rubber mallet. Mallets are not very expensive and they are worth having on hand.

Nail set
Nail sets are useful for any woodworking project because they help drive the nail a bit below the surface you have nailed, allowing you to fill the space with wood filler and stain or paint over the nail, rendering it invisible. The nail set should be slightly smaller than the nail you have used, which is why it's a good idea to buy a couple of nail sets, a small one and a medium-sized one. That way you can set small brads as well as larger nails.

SAFETY NOTE
Remember: Always use safety glasses when hammering!

NAILING IT!

Claw hammer
Don't be put off by the somewhat scary name: usually, people call this most useful of tools simply a hammer. That's because while there are several different kinds of hammers, this one is the most versatile and can perform most hammering and nail removal tasks you will face around the house.

A hammer's head drives nails into place, and its claw end prises out nails. It can also be used for other levering jobs. Despite the fact that claw hammers are easily found, they come in a variety of sizes, so choose one that feels good in your hand and isn't too big for you to wield forcefully without struggling. A 10-ounce version is good for many household repairs. But you can also find 13- and 16-ounce hammers, which are good for woodworking projects. A 16-ounce hammer may be too big and bulky for a lot of women to use, but you never know – you might prefer it. Try all three and see which one is best for you.

To use a nail set, simply hammer in the nail until the head just reaches the surface, then place the appropriate-sized nail set in the centre of the nail and tap it with your hammer until the nail is just slightly below the surface of the wood. Using your finger, patch the small hole with some wood filler.

Prybar
Sometimes the claw of a hammer just isn't long enough to give you the leverage that you need to prise a nail or other object away from the surface it's attached to. That's where a prybar comes in. The bar's length gives you the leverage you need to put pressure on one end to remove especially stubborn nails or screws. A 300-mm (12-in) prybar should be sufficient for most jobs. Larger versions of this tool are called wrecking bars or crowbars.

Staple gun
No woman should be without her gun – her staple gun, that is! Staple guns perform so many tasks, from re-covering the seat of a simple side chair to affixing latticework to a garden fence. Depending on the kind of staples you use, your gun can move easily from indoors to out. You can still buy

REACH THE PEAK OF SAFETY

Ladder use requires concentration and care. When working on a ladder, you have to focus both on what you are doing and be conscious that you are on a ladder. That means first and foremost removing all distractions when working on a ladder. Turning your head to answer a child's question or to shoo the cat out of the toolbox could spell disaster when you are balancing on high to hang a curtain rod or paint the coving. That means children, pets, television noise and anything else that could take your attention away should be kept out of the room you are working in. Here are some other tips that will keep you safe when on higher ground:

• Before placing a ladder, make sure the surface you are placing it on is free of debris and is level.
• Make sure a stepladder is unfolded all the way and the spreaders are completely rigid.
• Never, ever stand on the very top of a ladder!
• Keep your hips within the width of the ladder rails. Work from side to side only as far as your arms can reach without shifting your hips outside of the safety zone of the side rails. Never lean left or right out of that area; instead move the ladder to a better position.
• When moving your stepladder from place to place, collapse it. Never carry an unfolded ladder.
• Never, ever get on a ladder with another person. The rule is one person per ladder!

standard manual staple guns, but power electric or cordless guns are now available and are powerful yet easier to use. And some staple guns also allow you to switch over from staples to small brads, making light nailing jobs even easier.

Tack hammer

Tack hammers have standard handles but narrow heads, usually with a magnet on one side for holding tacks and brads. Upholsterers use tack hammers for tacking fabric, padding and lining to furniture and for driving decorative nail heads into furniture for a decorative and practical touch. Because a tack hammer is small and easy to control, it's also good for finer nailing jobs such as repairing a picture frame, where a standard hammer might damage the wood. A tack hammer can also get into tighter spaces than a regular hammer, so if you are hammering something at an odd angle, a tack hammer might be just the thing you need.

HIGHER GROUND

Stepladder

Don't skimp on a ladder. Buy the very best one you can afford, and use it only according to the manufacturer's instructions. Many household repairs and decorating jobs will require elevation of some kind. Please, please, don't use chairs, boxes or stacks of books to raise yourself up! This is so dangerous. Invest in a good metal or wooden folding stepladder. It slips

neatly into a broom cupboard or under your bed and is light enough to carry from room to room. Stepladders range from 1 to 4 m (3 to 12 ft). A 2-m (6-ft) ladder is a good choice for most households, although you may also want to buy a 1-m (3-ft) ladder for use in the kitchen. It's so much better than balancing on a chair when reaching for items stored high in your upper cabinets. A 2-m (6-ft) ladder will likely have a shelf for holding paint buckets or tools. Sometimes the shelf has an indentation for a bucket so that it has less of a chance of slipping off the shelf. Look for rugged hinges, a sturdy X brace on the rear legs, and rubber footings that will grip the floor and keep the ladder from moving around.

Extension ladder

An extension ladder is made up of two straight ladders with a brace that allows the user to extend the length. Extension ladders are usually used on larger construction sites and are not really necessary for most household jobs.

Folding ladder

There are two kinds of folding ladders: one is a stepladder that folds so it can be placed on surfaces of different heights, such as the floor and a stair tread. A folding straight ladder is similar to an extension ladder, except that it can also be folded over to resemble a stepladder.

TILE TIME

Grout float

A float is a rectangular plate with a handle on top and a rubber pad. It helps spread grout over tiles and stone smoothly and evenly. The rubber pad moves and packs the grout in between tiles, and it also wipes away excess grout – all in one fell swoop.

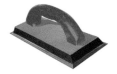

Notched spreader

This is a metal plate with a handle on top, which is notched on two sides. It is used for applying mastic or tile adhesive to large areas. The notches create ridges in the adhesive for good, even contact with the tile.

Putty knife

Putty knives come in a variety of sizes – from narrow to wide. Putty knives are not really knives at all; they are more

CENTIMETRE BY CENTIMETRE

There are two edges on every tape measure. One edge usually indicates inches divided into 16ths. The scale along the opposite edge has centimetres and millimetres. It allows you to mark off very precise measurements.

like metal spatulas, and you will find they have a variety of uses. For example, in masonry or tiling projects, you can use a putty knife to 'butter' the back of small pieces of tile with adhesive to fit in places that a notched spreader will not fit.

Steel trowel

Steel trowels are flat, metal, pie-shaped blades with a handle on one end. They are mainly used to do brickwork and may not be necessary for general household projects.

MEASURING UP

Tape measure

Most household projects require some form of measuring. Accurate measurements are essential to everything from hanging a picture to building a shelf to placing a sofa.

Flexible tape measures are handy for most measuring jobs, including calculating circumferences. In fact, I recommend carrying a tape measure with you whenever you are going to a flea market or going furniture shopping so you can measure larger items before you buy them.

The best tape measure to have is a metal retractable rule with a lock that allows you to hold it at a certain measure. A 10-m (30-ft) tape measure is most practical.

Folding ruler

Folding rulers are usually made out of wood. It may seem old-fashioned, but they are still being made, and they are useful. A folding ruler provides rigidity for measuring where a flexible tape measure might sag or fall over, such as measuring distances straight up over your head or beyond your arm's reach (and when there is no one available to hold the other end of a tape measure). Folding rulers usually unfold by 300-mm (1-ft) lengths up to 2.4 m (8 ft).

Carpenter's square

This type of ruler is used to draw 90-degree angles more than it is used for measuring. If you are interested in making your own mounts for picture frames or if you are planning on trying some woodworking projects, a carpenter's square is nice to have.

Compass

A compass is a metal device just like the one you used in school to draw circles. And that's what you can use it for today! You may want to cut a circle that's larger than what a drill bit can handle, so a compass is a good way of making a perfect circle, which you can then cut out with a pad or jigsaw. A compass is also good for scribing around edges that are not completely straight. For example, if you are cutting a piece of vinyl flooring to fit around a doorway, you can scribe the outline of the doorway and transfer it easily to your vinyl for a perfect fit.

Spirit level

A level helps you make sure your lines are straight and is particularly handy when hanging pictures, curtain rods and shelves. There are several kinds of levels, including technologically advanced laser levels that 'shoot' a line of light across an area. Technological advances aside, there are three basic kinds of levels: carpenter's, line and torpedo levels. Buy a level with both a horizontal and a vertical bubble.

A **carpenter's level** is rectangular and can run anywhere from 450 to 2400 mm (18 to 96 in) long! A length somewhere in between those two will be useful for most household projects. Look for a carpenter's level with at least three bubble windows: one in the centre for checking that things are level and one on either end for checking if a surface or edge is plumb. Windows that you can look at from above are very useful if you are working on floors or other surfaces where looking from the side would be impossible.

A **line level** is usually short (less than 300 mm/12 in) and has one centre bubble window. This level has two hooks on either end so it can be attached to a string. That makes it useful for outdoor projects or when levelling items that are far apart, such as checking that fence posts and railings are level.

A **torpedo level** is short, no more than 230 mm (9 in) long generally, and has three bubble windows, one in the middle and two flanking either side of the centre window. Its compact size makes it useful for checking level of pictures or small areas where a carpenter's level won't fit. Look for a torpedo level that lights up for easy viewing.

Chalk line

Chalk lines mark straight lines for applying moulding to walls, laying out garden paths or patios, and a host of other projects that require marking out long or large areas. A chalk line marker looks like an enclosed fishing reel. It has both string and chalk inside it. You pull it taut, with the help of a friend, and then snap it. Voilà! A chalk line will be created. Sometimes chalk line markers have hooks you can attach to a wall or a pole in the ground if extra hands are not available.

THE ART OF PAINTING

Bucket and tin pourer

Most DIY and paint stores sell buckets. It's a good idea to pour the paint you are using from its tin into a widemouthed paint bucket. Using a bucket instead of the tin eliminates

drips on the tin. When you use paint straight from the tin, the ridges in which the paint tin lid sits always get filled with paint, making it difficult to get the top on securely when you are done. DIY stores also sell plastic pouring rims that fit on paint tins, which make pouring into a bucket very neat as well.

Caulking (cartridge) gun

Small caulking jobs such as filling in nail holes in furniture before painting can be done with your finger. But bigger jobs, such as caulking around moulding or window frames, should be done with a caulking gun. These are inexpensive, and most caulk is sold in standard-size tubes that fit in the guns. If you have never used one before, practise first on newspaper to get a feel for it. The tube fits easily into the gun, and you apply pressure with the trigger. The trigger action automatically pushes a lever forward from the bottom of the tube, making sure the caulk is always pushed up to the top.

Paintbrushes

Paintbrushes come in all shapes and sizes to meet various painting needs. There are sash brushes for painting mouldings around windows and doors and large brushes for painting wide, flat areas. There are even small brushes for getting around thin chair legs and other small areas. And paintbrushes come with nylon and natural bristle.

Emulsion paint, which is now commonly used in all household applications because it is water-based, easy to clean up and more environmentally friendly than solvent-based paint, requires the use of nylon brushes. Natural brushes can only be used with solvent-based paint and can be costly. But many synthetic brushes are now made for use with solvent-based paints.

Even synthetic brushes can be expensive, so if you do invest in a good set of brushes, be sure to clean and dry them after each use and store them with the brush faces up so they do not break or stretch. I recommend buying four good all-purpose synthetic brushes in 25-, 50-, 75- and 100-mm (1-, 2-, 3-, and 4-in) widths. You can handle any small job with these brushes. Any large job should be done with a roller.

Paint mitts

Paint mitts are a fairly new invention. They are literally mitten-like gloves with palms that are covered in a material similar to a roller. They are useful if you are planning on painting a lot of stair spindles or chair legs, which can be

awkward to paint with a flat brush. The idea is to pour paint into a roller tray and put the palm of the glove (while you are wearing it) right into the paint lightly, so as not to drip. Then you can rub your mitted hand up and down the spindle or cylindrical object to paint it.

Paint pads

Paint pads have handles on top and are usually made of foam or mohair. They offer very smooth, even coverage over a large flat area. They take a little getting used to, however, and you might be just as well off using a roller for a large painting job.

Paint rollers

Rollers come is a variety of 'piles', which are chosen according to the surface you are painting. If you are painting brick, for example, you want a thicker, rougher pile that will help get the paint into all the nooks and crannies of the masonry. If you are painting plaster, you want a fine pile, which will achieve a smooth finish. If you are painting a large surface, such as a wall or ceiling, a roller is the way to go. Extension handles allow you to go right up a high wall or reach a ceiling with relative ease.

Paint tray and tray liner

Paint trays are made for use with a roller. A light plastic liner is a cheap way to keep the metal tray clean and to keep cleaning up to a minimum.

When you have finished painting, you can simply toss the liner away and wipe out the tray.

Painter's tape

Painter's tape is low-tack tape, meaning that it will not mar surfaces when you apply it to mask out areas that you do not want the paint to go. The tape is usually cream, but sometimes it can come in other colours. The adhesive on regular masking tape can stick to paint surfaces or, worse, tear them off when you remove the tape. So if you want to tape off surfaces (for example, around windows and doors before you paint moulding), always make sure you are using painter's tape. It is more expensive than regular masking tape, but it's worth the price because it saves having to repaint and repair a wall ruined by masking tape.

SANDPAPER AND SANDERS

Sandpaper is useful in the preparation of surfaces to be painted. Sandpaper comes in a variety of grits from very fine to very rough. Sandpaper is always numbered, and that number indicates the particle size of the grit. The higher the number of the sandpaper, the finer its particles will be and vice versa. Common grit categories and their uses are:

- 12 to 30 grit: very coarse, good for removing thick coats of paint or roughing up a metal or plastic surface to accept a base coat
- 36 to 50 grit: coarse, good for smoothing out surface imperfections on rough wood or for removing rust from metal
- 60 to 100 grit: medium, good for preliminary smoothing of wood surfaces in preparation for painting
- 120 to 180 grit: fine, good for final finishing of bare wood meant to be stained or painted and for sanding between coats of paint on wooded furniture and accessories
- 220 to 600 grit: very fine, good for smoothing and polishing finish paint and stain or polyurethane coats on wood and metal

Use sandpaper as is for small jobs or use a sanding block, electric palm sander or belt sander for bigger projects. A **sanding block** is easy to handle on medium-sized surfaces, such as a tabletop. An **electric palm sander** is useful for sanding tables and furniture and will be less tiring to use than a block. It's small enough to, like the name says, fit in your hand or palm. A **belt sander** is good for sanding large items such as doors. It's heavier than an electric palm sander, making it more unwieldy to use. You can also get smaller or specialized electric sanders that fit in small spaces.

No matter what kind of sandpaper you use or what kind of device you use it with, sand wood in the direction of the grain; otherwise you will mar the surface, and it will be difficult to repair.

Steel wool comes in similar grades of abrasion as sandpaper and can also be used for sanding purposes. Very fine grade steel wool, which comes in flat, thin pads or the more familiar-looking pillows, can be used for removing, polishing and cleaning finishes, and for sanding between coats of finish and paint. They are especially useful on furniture projects. Coarse grade steel wool can be used for cleaning rust off metal objects. For example, if you are repainting outdoor metal or wrought-iron furniture, a good scrub with a steel wool pad will remove loose surface rust and prepare the surface for a coat of metal primer.

Paint scraper

You use a paint scraper to prepare wall surfaces for painting. It helps get rid of bumps and dried drips of paint that can prevent you from achieving a smooth look to your new paint job. And remember, in painting as in life, preparation is everything! Most scrapers are plastic, but at a push you could use a wide metal putty knife to remove any bumps from your wall.

Wallpaper scoring tool

This small, round device has many little blades that score wallpaper for easier removal. The scoring allows water to penetrate the paper and soften the wallpaper paste faster. Simply run the tool in big circles across the wallpapered area and then spray or wet down the wallpaper with a sponge. The wallpaper should, once the paste is softened, scrape off with a little elbow grease. You can also rent a wallpaper steamer, which helps to make short work of wallpaper removal as well.

Wire brush

Wire brushes are good for removing old paint from metal and wood surfaces, especially in hard-to-reach places such as between spindles and chair legs. Be sure to sand the area you brushed with the metal bristle, however, because it can leave little grooves in whatever you have brushed.

TAKE THE PLUNGE

Hand auger

A hand auger is like a snake that spools back into its reel so you don't have to touch it. This is a useful item if there is something blocking your sink and the plunger doesn't help. There is a spiral hook at the end of the auger that will push through a grease, soap or food blockage and clear the pipe. To use a hand auger (which may not come with instructions), push the flexible

snake into the drain until you feel the blockage. Tighten the locknut and turn the handle clockwise while pushing on the body. The spiral hook will either loosen the blockage and bore through it, or it will grab onto the cause of the blockage so you can retrieve it.

WC auger

This auger is meant specifically for use in the toilet. (So don't be tempted to use it in the kitchen sink!) It works on the same principle as the hand auger – by

moving or fishing out whatever is causing the blockage and clearing a path in the drain.

Pipe wrench

Pipe wrenches are often used in pairs to loosen or tighten pipe connections. That's because you don't want the pipe to turn while you are turning the fitting – because you might not see what the turning pipe is actually affecting inside a wall or beneath the floor. Hold one wrench to keep the pipe in place and use the other wrench to grip and turn the fitting.

Plunger

A good old-fashioned rubber plunger can get rid of most minor sink and toilet blockages. Recommendation: buy a funnel-cup plunger because they have more power than standard cup plungers. And buy two: one for sink use and the other for toilet use.

SEE SAW

Tenon saw and mitre box

A tenon saw has a rigid spine that stiffens its back, making it fairly inflexible. It is designed to make straight cuts across the

grain of wood and is most often used in a mitre box. Mitre boxes make it very easy to accomplish very straight cuts at 45- or 90-degree angles. That's perfect if you want to make mitre-cut frames or moulding. Mitre boxes are made in either wood or plastic, and some have a variety of slots or different angle cuts.

Coping saw

A coping saw is normally used to make fine cuts with sharp curves. Its replaceable blade is flexible, very thin and extremely sharp. Depending on the blade you use, you can cut wood, plastic or metal with a coping saw. It's excellent for cutting the scribed edge of moulding.

Crosscut saw

A crosscut saw is most useful for cutting wood. As the name implies, it is used most effectively by cutting across the grain of the wood. So, for example,

this is a good saw to use to cut lengths of larger pieces of wood. You can also use this saw to cut plywood, which has grain going in both directions.

Hacksaw

Hacksaws are commonly used for cutting through metal, such as a thin pipe. They can also cut through wood and plastic. You can buy blades that range in size from 200 to 300 mm (8 to 12 in), and the saw adjusts to fit the blade size.

Keyhole saw

Keyhole saws (also known as padsaws) are meant to cut curves and are especially useful when cutting through plasterboard. Electricians use keyhole saws to cut out holes for recessed lights in ceilings, for instance.

Opposite: Sawhorses help cut down on the potential messiness of many painting and staining jobs.

Jigsaw

Jigsaws are wonderful power saws that are easy to operate with just a little practice. They are extremely useful for all sorts of projects that involve wood. The saw's blade cuts at varying speeds, and you can easily cut circular and linear shapes with one. Because they are so popular, a quality jigsaw can be had at a very reasonable price. The blades are inexpensive enough that you can replace them when they become blunt.

There are other power saws, such as circular saws, that I did not include on this list. They are dangerous tools that need a certain amount of practice and training before you feel comfortable using them. Some home improvement superstores offer classes in how to use these saws. I urge you to take such a class if you are interested in learning how to use these powerful cutting tools.

ETC.

Block plane

A block plane is a wood chisel that is set into a body that allows you to control how much wood is removed from the surface you're working on. This can be used to plane down cabinet or bureau doors that are stuck or even stubborn wooden cupboard or bedroom doors. Practice makes perfect, however. So I recommend perfecting your technique and control on a scrap piece of wood before you tackle your bulging front door!

Sawhorses

Two sawhorses are essential equipment if you are going to get serious about home improvement projects. Set up across from each other, two sawhorses can support material you are working on, such as a long piece of wood. Or you can place a piece of plywood or a hollow-core door across them to create a temporary table or workstation. Sawhorses can be bought at any DIY store. They are made of wood, metal, heavy duty plastic or a combination of those materials. They can usually be folded up flat for storage.

Have Tools, Will Travel

Tools are accessories for living. There are a handful of tools I consider essential for every woman to have: a hammer, pliers, wrench, screwdriver, tape measure, level and a set of Allen keys. If you have those nearby, you are well on your way to home repair victory.

A basic tool kit will include just a few more useful tools and materials. But before you go out and buy everything or anything on the following three lists, check out what you already own. Do you like them? Do they feel good in your hands? Do you want to use them? Keep what you like and what works for you, donate what doesn't (but may be good for someone else), and toss or recycle the rest (anything broken, damaged, rusted or blunt and therefore useless).

Barbara K's Basic Tool Kit

These tools and materials should be part of your household tool arsenal. This may seem like a long list, but many of these items are inexpensive and don't take up a lot of room.

TOOLS

- Adjustable spanner
- Allen, or hex, keys in various sizes
- Buckets in a range of sizes
- Bungee cords
- Carpenter's square
- C-clamp
- Claw hammer with soft grip
- Compass
- Hacksaw
- Long nose pliers
- Nail set
- Paintbrushes (four to six in a variety of sizes, from small artist brushes to standard wall paint brushes, in both natural and synthetic bristle)
- Paint pads
- Paint roller with rolls
- Paint scraper
- Paint tray
- Power drill with a set of drill and screw bits
- Prybar
- Putty knife
- Safety goggles (plastic)
- Sawhorses
- Screwdrivers (four flat-tip sizes and two pozidriv drivers) or a 6-in-1 interchangeable screwdriver
- Sink plunger
- Slip joint pliers
- Spirit level
- Spring clamps (small and medium)
- Staple gun with staples
- Step ladder
- Tape measure
- Tenon saw and mitre box
- Utility knife with replacement blades
- Wallpaper scoring tool
- Wire brush
- Wood chisels

ADVANCED TOOL KIT

Add these items to the list above, and you'll have an awesome bag of tricks up your sleeve!
- Bench vice
- Block plane
- Caulking gun
- Chalk line
- Cold chisel
- Combination square
- Coping saw
- Crosscut saw
- Crowbar
- Jigsaw and spare blades
- Keyhole saw
- Knee pads
- Mallet
- Metal snips or metal shears
- Notched spreader
- Pipe wrench
- Power sander with various grades of sandpaper
- Sink auger
- Steel trowel
- Stud finder (unfortunately, this won't help you find a man, but it will impress one if you can use it!)
- Tack hammer
- WC auger
- Web clamps

MATERIALS

- Carpet tape
- Duct tape
- Dust sheets
- Extension flex
- Flooring adhesive
- Glazing points (brads)
- Glue gun and glue sticks
- Instant-grip adhesive (one brand is called Liquid Nails)
- Mesh repair tape
- Nails in a variety of types and sizes
- Painter's tape
- Penetrating oil
- Plaster filler
- Rags (clean and soft)
- Sanding block and sandpaper in various grits
- Screws in a variety of sizes and finishes including steel and brass
- Sponges
- Spray adhesive
- Spray bottle
- Stain-block primer
- Stain sticks
- Steel wool in a variety of grades
- Stencils
- Tap O-rings
- Tap washers
- Tile adhesive
- Tile grout
- Velcro strips
- Wallpaper paste
- White woodworking adhesive
- Wood filler
- White spirit

The Walls Around You

Walls, whether they're made from plasterboard, plaster, wood, stone or masonry, represent something that both surrounds and divides us. Walls are a huge part of life; they provide privacy and shelter no matter where you are – at home, in the office, even when you're on holiday. Think about what goes into making a wall: there's a great deal of intricacy in the building of a stone wall, for instance. And even the simplest sheet of plasterboard won't stay up without the assistance of the studs that support it.

Walls and ceilings offer the most opportunities for simple yet dramatic change. By enhancing walls with any of the finishes available – from paint to wallpaper – and embellishing them with artwork and photographs, you can make a space your own, express your style and display what makes you happy. In doing this, you will completely transform a room.

Even better: wall and ceiling projects are among the easiest of home improvement and decorating jobs to accomplish. Best of all? Most wall and ceiling fixes will give you immediate results, helping to build your confidence to take on more challenging projects.

SAFETY NOTES

Remember always to follow the manufacturer's instructions when using any product, even if you have used it in the past. Manufacturers take a lot of time to write user-friendly instructions, and they know better than anyone how to use their particular materials or tools. Also remember when embarking on any wall or ceiling project to work in a room that's been cleared of any breakable or moving objects. (That means no Ming vases or Rollerblades, please.)

If you can't move a piece of furniture because it's too big, cover it with a dust sheet to protect it. Even if you are working in a small area, protect adjacent surfaces or move them out of the way. That kind of preparation can save future heartbreak. You don't want to repair or paint a wall only to find that you've dropped filler on your sideboard.

When working with paint and filler, always work in a well-ventilated room. Keep windows and doors open! Wear a mask if you are kicking up a lot of dust, for example sanding down plaster patches. Wear safety glasses if you are working on your ceiling or with any material that spatters. Clean up and dispose of chemicals, paint, plaster and other materials according to the manufacturers' recommendations. And please follow your local environment rules for product disposal.

The Pleasure of Paint

Painting is a relatively easy and quick way of breathing new life into a room. The key to achieving a professional look on your own, however, is preparation. Taking a little extra time to ready a room for painting will pay off big time once you get started. And learning about the different kinds of paint and the kind of effects they can achieve is essential. There are so many ways to achieve paint finishes available these days, and each one will result in a different mood, texture and reflective quality.

I love colours, and luckily there are many of them to choose from today. If you don't like any of the vast range of ready-mixed paint colours available, you have the option of bringing in your favourite sweater or skirt, scarf or vintage image for a computer colour match. The creative options are endless. And once you have painted a room, believe me, you'll be bitten by the home improvement bug forever.

I'll spare you the scientific details of paint composition. Basically, paint is a combination of colour (pigment) and a binder that allows it to be spread evenly on a surface. But there are certain terms you should know because they will help you choose the right paint for the project.

BEFORE YOU SHOP FOR PAINT

There's nothing I hate more than trekking back to the DIY store for another tin of paint because I didn't buy enough in the first place. Measuring the surfaces you are planning on painting will eliminate annoying extra trips to the paint department. It's a simple process, but don't worry if you wind up with a bit more paint than you need. It's smart to have extra paint on hand for touch-ups later on. For example, if you have to repair a patch in a wall, you'll be able to repaint it easily with the leftovers you have on hand.

The surface you will be painting, its condition and original colour, as well as the type of paint you want to use will have an impact on the quantity of paint you will need. The basic rule is 1 litre of paint per 15 sq m of wall space. However, if you are going from a dark colour to a light colour, or vice versa, you will likely have to buy a tinted primer in the same quantity. Using a tinted primer will usually allow you to get away with only one coat of paint. But if you are painting a room a very dark colour, say a deep red or midnight blue, you may have to use a tinted primer and double the amount of paint you use. You will probably need to give the walls two or three coats to get the true, deep colour you're after.

Paint Types

Here are the basic types of paint you're likely to encounter.

ACRYLIC: Acrylic paint is a water-based paint commonly used in small painting jobs and craft projects. You can buy it in small bottles in craft stores. It's excellent for painting small details on furniture and accessories. If you find a colour of acrylic paint you love, you can have the DIY store make a match with emulsion paint.
Brush fuss: Use synthetic or foam brushes.

EMULSION: Emulsion paint is popular for its ease of use. Emulsion paints are water-based and have low fumes. Cleaning up can be done with liquid soap and water. And dried paint can usually be peeled off of a paint bucket and roller tray and thrown away. Manufacturers have improved the quality and durability of interior and exterior emulsion paints over the years. Just be sure you are buying the correct one for the job. You might choose to use gloss emulsion in bathroom and kitchen applications because it has protective water-resistant qualities.
Brush fuss: Use synthetic brushes.

SOLVENT-BASED: Solvent-based or alkyd paint is thick and sticky, making it somewhat difficult to work with. It also has a strong smell. You absolutely must work in a well-ventilated room when working with any solvent-based product. It also requires special products for cleaning up, such as paint thinners (another smelly and often dangerous chemical). Because manufacturers have made such great strides in emulsion paint quality and durability, I don't think you need to use solvent-based paint for most jobs. But gloss solvent-based paints, which were commonly used in kitchens and bathrooms because of their water-resistant quality, have a sheen and reflective quality that gloss emulsion paint just can't match. So if you are dead set on a certain finish (we'll talk about paint finishes in detail later in this chapter), solvent-based gloss may be the only way to go.

You can also buy solvent-based paints formulated for use on hot surfaces, such as ovens, exposed hot water pipes and radiators. Many spray paints are made specifically for appliances, as well. And there are paints

BARBARA'S BEST-KEPT SECRET

If you are doing a painting job over a weekend and using solvent-based paint, you can wait until the very end to clean up the brushes with paint thinners by using this simple mid-process storage trick. Wrap the paintbrushes in aluminium foil, place them in a plastic storage bag and put the whole thing in the freezer. The brushes will stay pliant and the paint won't freeze. You can go right back to painting and then clean the brushes out when the job is completely done!

suitable for painting over tile and porcelain that simulate a ceramic finish. The upside to solvent-based paint is its durability, especially on window frames and in kitchens and bathrooms. Today's solvent-based paint is easier to clean, and newer formulations make it less likely to yellow over time. *Brush fuss:* Use natural-bristle brushes.

SPRAY PAINT: Spray paint is solvent-based and perfect for garden furniture, wrought iron and almost anything that's made of metal. They even make spray paint that will cover plastic without peeling. Spray paint is easy to use and does not require the preparation work that paint in a tin demands.

PRIMER: Primer is used to prepare surfaces for paint. 'Raw' plasterboard needs to be covered with plasterboard primer before paint goes on top. Primer basically readies the board to accept paint. Primer can also be used when going from a dark to a light colour or vice versa. In those cases, you want to ask your paint mixer to create a tinted primer with a colour close to but not exactly like the topcoat. This will reduce the number of coats you have to give your wall or ceiling. Primer is also essential if you are covering a solvent-based paint with an emulsion paint. A primer will create a suitable surface for the new covering. If you leave out that step, the emulsion paint will pull right off the oil-based surface. Ugh!

You don't always have to use primer: if you are painting flat beige or off-white walls, you can generally go right over the paint with your new colour.

Paint Finishes

These are the different types of paint finishes you have to choose from.

FLAT: This matt surface paint finish is usually used on interior walls. It helps hide small imperfections because it doesn't reflect light. (Shinier paint highlights imperfections.) Flat paint is generally hard to clean or scrub, but some manufacturers are making flat paints that are washable. Still, you have to be cautious when cleaning a flat-painted wall.

EGGSHELL: This finish has just a whisper of sheen. You could hardly call it shiny. It's good for interior walls, especially if you have kids running around, simply because you will have an easier time cleaning it than a flat-painted wall. However, an eggshell finish still looks somewhat matt, and any imperfections will remain subtle if not invisible.

SATIN: This smooth, somewhat shiny paint is perfect for children's rooms because it's so easy to clean. Kitchens, bathrooms and high-traffic areas also benefit from a satin finish because it holds up under light scrubbing.

SEMI-GLOSS: Semi-gloss paint is most often used on doors, mouldings and cabinets in kitchens and bathrooms. It's easy to keep clean, and its subtle shine is rich looking and especially crisp on mouldings when set against a flat-painted wall. Surface preparation is important, though, because semi-gloss will show imperfections. So be sure to fill all holes and gouges, smooth surfaces and sand mouldings to be painted. Get rid of built-up paint layers and dried drips, too.

GLOSS: Gloss paints are super-shiny. Most people don't use them on interior walls, although I have seen ceilings in gloss, and the reflection is amazing. Gloss can also look very fresh on wall panelling and on cabinets, mouldings and furniture, especially in contemporary settings. A front door painted in high gloss looks stylish and formal, especially when done in a dark colour such as forest green or even black. A warning: gloss paint highlights every surface imperfection, so be sure your surface is completely smooth before using a high-gloss paint.

Other Paint Terms

These are two more paint terms you need to know to be a painting pro.

CUTTING IN: This simply means painting around doors, windows, mouldings and skirting boards with an appropriate brush. After you've completed cutting in, you do the rest of the wall-painting job with a roller.

KEY: This slight roughness to a surface allows it to accept paint. For example, if you are planning on painting over a glossy surface, even if it's with more glossy paint, you have to prime it first to give the surface a key, which will accept the new paint. Otherwise, the paint will peel off.

What Colour Is Your Paint Tin?

I love colour! It can bring such joy and energy to your surroundings. But with so many colours to choose from, how will you know if a colour, which may look pretty under the florescent glare of the DIY shop lights, is really right for you? You won't, unless you buy a sample and test it on a piece of scrap material that's been primed the same way as the surface you're intending to paint. A paint chip just doesn't cut it when it comes to seeing how a colour will act once it's covering all four walls. Many paint manufacturers now offer sample pots to cover a small area of wall.

Here's a great way to pinpoint your favourite shade. Buy one sample pot in three shades of the same colour: one light, one medium and one dark. Once you get your samples on the wall, live with them for a week. Check the room at various times of day to see how the colour has changed. Do you still like it? Which tones do you like best? Also keep in mind when you will

The same colour can be mixed in different tones. Try more than one shade of your chosen colour before you make a final decision.

be most using the room you're painting. During the day? At night? Those are the times of day to pay the most attention to how the colour looks.

The next consideration is the type of surface you'll be painting, whether it be plasterboard, plaster, brick or stone. There is not a lot of difference between painting plaster and plasterboard surfaces. 'Raw' or unfinished plasterboard needs to be primed before it is painted. Other than that, painting plasterboard is a breeze. (Follow the directions in the 'Paint a Wall' project on page 53.) Painting plaster is the same as painting plasterboard. And if you have a newly plastered wall, it is important to prime it first (just as you would with brand new plasterboard) to prepare the surface for a topcoat of paint. It's also a good idea to prime patches before repainting, otherwise the patch colour may not match the rest of the wall.

Masonry can be painted with emulsion paint, but some preparation is required. Brick or stone must be cleaned with a stiff wire brush, and any dust has to be removed with the long hose of a vacuum cleaner before painting. Missing pointing has to be repaired. The surface has to be primed with a self-sealing primer and then painted with either a long-pile roller (to get into all the nooks and crannies) or a large brush to work the paint into the surface further. Expect to do two coats.

Here's a masonry-painting trick that you may not have thought of: instead of painting the outside of your fireplace, consider painting the inside of it with a heat resistant, flat, black, solvent-based paint made specifically to endure temperatures up to 500°C (available at any home improvement or paint specialist). The black paint will make soot invisible. When the fireplace is not in use, the black interior lessens the empty appearance of the fireback. It's sleek and elegant!

My fireback went from gloomy to glamorous with just a lick of paint!

Get Inspired!

CREATE AN INSPIRATION BOARD
Time: About 1 hour

Before you paint and decorate a room, create an inspiration board. It will help sort out your thoughts and inspire you to create new colour and style combinations. It's a useful decorating tool that's super easy and fun to make.

WHAT YOU NEED
Magazines and books, photos or other images
Paint chips
Fabric, carpet and tile samples, if applicable
Glue stick or glue gun and glue
Foam core board (available at craft stores)

HOW TO GET IT DONE
1. Let it rip! Go through your favourite decorating magazines and catalogues and clip out any pictures you love. It can be a photo of an entire interior, a piece of furniture or an accessory, a texture (think wood floor) or even a colour! A favourite photo of the beach or autumn leaves can inspire a room. Collect fabric and swatches, paint chips and carpet samples; you can even pick up tile samples. Gather them together, and chances are you will see a pattern of colours and styles emerge.
2. Next, lay out the clippings, samples and swatches in the general order of the room. Glue the carpet sample or photo on the bottom of the foam core board. Then attach fabric samples and furniture and accessory images in the middle of the board. Paint chips can be glued in a fan next to furnishings. Attach curtain material or images near the top of the board. This will give you a much clearer idea than sticking samples randomly over the board. Inspirational photos can be stuck to the sides. Try cutting out extra pieces of foam core and sticking images on them to create a 3-D effect on your board. This three-dimensional quality will give life to your collage.
3. Take this board with you when you shop for your room. It will keep you focused and on track. Make one for every room in your house!

Opposite: *An inspiration board is a great way to organize your ideas and keep your decorating project focused.*

Preparing for Painting

Okay. You've selected a dreamy colour and bought it in just the right amount. Now you're ready to plunge in and make some changes. First things first: your outfit. Wear comfortable clothes you don't care about because you will, I guarantee, get paint on your shirt, trousers and shoes, which could become your new fashion statement. A well-worn T-shirt, old jeans and dirty trainers with good rubber soles are appropriate choices.

Next clear out the room you will be painting and cover any surfaces you can't move. Consolidate pictures, books, lamps, accessories and other small items into a bin so they don't go missing. Move heavy furniture into the centre of the room if you can't take it out of the space. Cover all remaining items, and the floor, with dust sheets. Inexpensive plastic ones are perfect for covering furniture, but they are not good for protecting the floor because they are slippery. *Do not cover the floor with a plastic dust sheet!* Use a heavy-duty canvas dust sheet for the floor. They are not expensive, and they last forever.

Once your room is cleared and protected, remove everything you can from the walls. Unscrew switch plate covers, curtain hardware and doorknobs. If you don't want to take off the doorknob, tape off the knob completely with masking tape. Keep all the bits and pieces in a plastic storage bag and place it in your accessory bin. Then tape off the mouldings with painter's tape. It's low tack and won't rip off paint when you remove it.

Open the doors and windows. Even if it's cold outside, put on a sweatshirt and open windows at least a crack, just to keep fresh air flowing in the room. The point is not to close off the room. Any fumes will be reduced and the room will dry faster.

Go around the room and fill any small holes and cracks with joint compound. It's easy: using a putty knife or even your finger, spread the joint compound into the small hole or crack. (We'll talk about bigger holes later in this chapter.) When the compound is dry, sand it down until it's smooth. Better yet, instead of sanding, use the contractor's trick of gently rubbing the spot with a damp sponge in a circular motion. This will cut down on the texture that sandpaper can sometimes create, leaving you with a less visible repair.

Use a scraper to remove any bumps or dried paint drips. While you are waiting for the filler to dry (no more than 30 minutes), gather your materials together and place them in one easy-to-reach area.

Put Some Colour in Your Life, Starting with Your Walls

PAINT A WALL

Time: At least 1 full day to an entire weekend, depending on the size
and intricacy of the job

Painting a room can take a good chunk of time but it's such a simple,
satisfying project that I hope you'll try it. And please don't do standard
beige – experiment with a favourite light, happy colour or a warm romantic
tone. It's worth taking a chance on colour because it's easy to paint over if
you don't like it at the end. Chances are, after you live with your choice for
a week, you'll love it!

WHAT YOU NEED

Painter's tape
Bins for storage
Dust sheets
Primer
Appropriate rollers and brushes (long-pile rollers for textured or stucco walls, short
   pile for plasterboard and smooth plaster walls, 25- to 50-mm angled-tip brushes
   for trim, 75- to 100-mm straight-tip brushes for walls)
Flat-tip screwdriver
Stirring sticks
Paint
Nail
Hammer
Plastic paint bucket or roller paint trays with liners
Extension pole for rollers
Stepladder
Utility knife
Rags and sponges
Paint thinners, a mask and rubber gloves (if using solvent-based paint)

HOW TO GET IT DONE

1. Once the walls are prepared, surfaces not to be painted are covered with painter's tape, accessories are stored in bins and furniture still in the room is covered with dust sheets. Prime the walls if necessary using both a brush and a roller. Cut in around doors and windows and around trim mouldings. Remember, you only have to prime if you are going from one colour extreme to another or if you are moving from a solvent-based paint to an emulsion paint. Primer doesn't take long to dry – about an hour. Test it first, however, before applying the finish coat.

2. Open your paint tin with a flat-tip screwdriver and stir the paint from the bottom using a stirring stick. I make small holes around the rim by piercing it with a nail and hammer. It might seem like this would allow the paint to spill, but the small holes actually allow the poured paint to drip back into the can and reduce the amount of paint that sits and dries in the can's top ridge. Pour the paint into a plastic bucket and/or roller paint tray (lined with a cheap plastic liner you can toss out when you're done).

3. Begin painting with a 75- or 100-mm (3- or 4-in) brush and cut in around all doors, skirting boards and windows. Don't dip more than one-third of the brush into the paint. Remove excess by tapping the side of the brush on the bucket. Don't wipe it down – that will remove too much paint.

4. A roller will make short work of large expanses of wall. Once you have painted all around woodwork, get your roller ready. Rolling will reduce paintbrush marks and result in a smooth finish. Placing the end of the roller in an expansion pole allows you to reach to the top of the wall without having to get on a ladder. However, you will need to stand on a ladder to paint around the top of the wall or tape off the ceiling. Whether you are painting large areas with a roller or a brush, paint in a crosshatch or M pattern.

5. When painting mouldings, go slowly and try to be as precise as possible. Don't worry too much if you get paint on a glass window. It can be easily scraped off with the edge of your utility knife.

6. If you are painting a ceiling, an extension rod will make the job much easier. Use a ladder (check out ladder safety tips in 'Reach the Peak of Safety' on page 31) to cut in at least 75 to 100 mm (3 to 4 in) where the ceiling meets the wall. Then complete the job with a roller on an

extension pole. Instead of rolling the paint on a ceiling in an M pattern, use a W pattern. Start at the outside edge of the ceiling and work your way up and down the length of the room. Take breaks; even with a long pole, painting a ceiling is tough on your neck and shoulders. Use a damp rag or sponge to quickly wipe up any paint splatters.

Enjoy the process. Be mindful of what you're doing. With every stroke of the brush, every turn of the roller, you are improving your room and your life. Just think how much better you'll feel in a room full of colour, colour that you picked out and that you put on the walls yourself.

Wait at least 48 hours after painting a wall before putting anything on your newly painted walls, to ensure that everything is completely dry. Keep the dust sheet down so any paint or water drops can dry. Then fold it up and store it away.

Finally, don't put off cleaning up! Clean the rim of the paint tin first, before replacing the lid. Cover any remaining paint in the tin with a piece of plastic wrap. This will hinder the formation of a 'skin'. If there is only a small amount of paint left, pour it into a smaller container, such as a glass jar with a tight fitting lid, and mark it with the paint's brand name, colour and number.

Good brushes will last forever if you clean them properly. Simply wash emulsion paint brushes in warm soapy water and rinse them in the sink until the water runs clear. Dry them with a paper towel and store with bristles facing up. If you have used solvent-based paint, you will need to clean your brushes with paint thinners and a rag (wear gloves!) and then run them under water to rinse. Follow the instructions on the paint tin for best and safest results. Pat the brushes dry with paper towels and store with bristles upright.

Check with your local authority waste disposal department about local paint disposal rules – and follow them!

OUT OF ORDER!
If you are painting everything in a room, do it in order. Start with the ceiling first, then walls, doors and mouldings. If you are painting the floor, do that last and, whatever happens, don't paint yourself into a corner!

TROUBLE IN PARADISE

Even the pros can run into painting predicaments. Here are some savvy solutions for common problems:

AIR BUBBLES: This usually happens when solvent-based gloss paint is applied in bright sunlight or on water-based undercoats. The paint should be removed, the area primed and then it should be painted out of the direct sun. (Pull the curtains but keep the window open!)

BLISTERS: This can be caused by moisture when exposed to the sun. Scrape off the blister, sand it down and repaint.

BRUSH BRISTLE IN YOUR PAINT: I hate it when this happens! Which is why it's a good idea to invest in high quality brushes. Cheaper brushes have a tendency to shed. But even the best brushes release a little bristle once in a while. If that happens, don't try to pick it out of the wet paint with your fingers. Very gently pick up the bristle with the very edge of the brush and then remove it from the brush with your fingers.

CHIPPING: This is often caused by the top coat not having a sufficient key. It usually happens when painting on top of an unprimed gloss finish. The only way to prevent this is to prime the gloss surface first or sand the gloss surface down with fine sandpaper and repaint.

COLOUR NOT ALL THE SAME SHADE: You may not have stirred the paint properly. Paint should be stirred thoroughly from the bottom before use.

CRACKLING: This happens when old solvent-based paint has hardened and is unable to expand and contract with changing weather conditions. Small crackling can be sanded down, primed and repainted. Severe crackling on a piece of furniture should be stripped back to bare wood, then primed and repainted.

MILDEW: Remove mildew with a mixture of bleach and water (2 parts water to 1 part bleach) and a sponge. Mildew on walls appears because of moisture in the area. Identify and fix the moisture problem before painting.

RUNNY PAINT: Slow down! Applying paint too heavily normally causes runs. Don't overload your brush with paint. And if runs and drips do happen, brush them out before the paint sets.

Get Plastered

If you live in a home built before 1950, the chances are very good that your walls are made from lath-and-plaster – strips of wood or metal that provide a means of holding plaster in place. Creating a plaster wall is a pretty labour-intensive job, which is one reason why it's not done any more. It's just much too expensive. But for those of you who live in older homes, getting to know your plaster walls will help you solve minor plaster problems when they happen.

Lath strips were first covered with a coarse layer of plaster called a scratch coat. The wet plaster squeezed through the gaps in the lath, locking it to the walls and ceiling. If you have ever seen a hole in a plaster wall, you know what I'm talking about. It looks like cake icing that's dried in between the strips of wood. After the scratch coat dried, a second browning coat was applied to make the surfaces rough but flat. When this layer was dry, the final coat, called a skim coat, was then carefully placed on the wall in a thin layer.

Consider yourself lucky to have plaster walls. They are historical and are evidence of great craftspeople of the past. It took a tremendous amount of skill to create a smooth, even plaster wall.

Today, you will often see a skim coat of plaster spread smoothly on top of plasterboard to replicate a plaster look. It can also be spread on top of brick or stone. It takes years of training and practice to become good at plastering and producing a fine skim coat. But minor repairs are completely doable, and the materials needed are inexpensive and common. It's important to know a few quick plaster fixes, because if you want to paint plaster walls, cracks and holes must be filled and sanded first.

If your plaster problems are major, however, you must call in professional help. For example, if a plaster ceiling looks like it's falling down, it just might be. So use caution and hire a pro to demolish it and replace it with plasterboard. Furthermore, if there are major cracks in plaster walls, the building may have severe settling problems or water damage. All houses settle, but big cracks may indicate a serious structural problem, which you should investigate further.

DEFINING MOMENT

BROWNING COAT: This is the second, rough coat of plaster.

CORNER BEAD: This wire mesh with a rigid metal spine is used on outside corners.

JOINT COMPOUND: This is a plaster-like substance that is used to fill seams and irregularities in plasterboard or plaster.

LATH: Lath strips, which can be made from wood or metal, provide a means of holding plaster in place.

SCRATCH COAT: This is the first coat of plaster set over lath.

SKIM COAT: This is the final plaster coat. It creates a lovely smooth, flat finish.

Patchwork

PATCH A SMALL CRACK IN PLASTER

Time: 30 minutes, plus drying time

Have you ever taken down a curtain rod or a picture, only to be faced with unsightly holes left behind by the nails or screws or a crack that was hidden before? That happened to me when I raised the height of my curtains in my living room. But filling the small holes was easy. And when I was done, no one could tell that the rod had been moved from one spot to another.

WHAT YOU NEED

Safety glasses
Mask
Flat-tip screwdriver
Clean, soft-bristle paintbrush
Fine sandpaper

Joint compound
Narrow putty knife
Primer and paint in your wall or
  ceiling colour
Paintbrush

HOW TO GET IT DONE

1. If the crack is in the ceiling, wear safety glasses and a mask.
2. Using the tip of your screwdriver, widen the crack so that you can apply patching material in it. Be sure to brush away any loose material with a clean, soft-bristle paintbrush.
3. Sand down the edges of the open crack with fine sandpaper.
4. Use a narrow putty knife to spread joint compound along the length of the crack. Push it into the opening and feather it out around the crack. Make it as smooth as possible. If your wall has a stucco effect, mimic the texture by pulling the putty knife straight up to create peaks.
5. Allow the compound to dry. Depending on the weather and humidity levels, this could take anywhere from an hour or so to 24 hours.
6. Sand the area with fine sandpaper until it is completely smooth. Skip this step if you have a textured effect.
7. Prime the spot. Plaster is absorbent, and priming will help the finish paint coat maintain the same colour as the rest of the wall. When the primer is dry, paint the wall.

PATCH A LARGE CRACK IN PLASTER
Time: 40 minutes, plus drying time

Patching a large crack is similar to filling a small crack. As before, wear safety glasses and a mask if the crack is in the ceiling. Be sure to open the crack wide enough so that all loose plaster is removed and you reach stable plaster (and don't forget to brush away any loose material). Now follow steps 3 to 7 of 'Patch a Small Crack in Plaster' on the opposite page. If the crack is very large, a lot of wet joint compound may not want to stick. If that is the case, complete the process with the following material and steps:

WHAT YOU NEED
Self-adhesive mesh repair tape
Wide putty knife

HOW TO GET IT DONE
1. Cover the crack with a length of tape.
2. Using a putty knife, cover the tape with joint compound.
3. Squeeze out any excess compound by pressing the putty knife along the tape. Make sure there are no lumps in the patch.
4. Let the patch dry. Larger patches will take longer to dry than small ones.
5. Sand lightly.
6. Prime and paint.

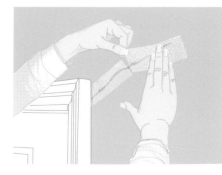

Step 1. Cover the crack with tape.

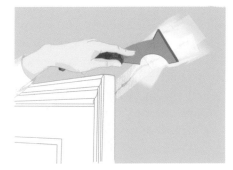

Step 2. Cover tape with joint compound.

Power Patching

. . . .

PATCH SMALL, MEDIUM AND LARGE HOLES
Time: 40 minutes, plus drying time

Holes in plaster can be fixed in a similar fashion to cracks, but you will need more patching material.

WHAT YOU NEED
Rubber gloves
Safety glasses
Mask
Flat-tip screwdriver
Clean, soft-bristle paintbrush
PVA bonding liquid
Paintbrush
Joint compound
Wide putty knife
Fine sandpaper
Primer and paint in your wall or ceiling colour
Paintbrush

HOW TO GET IT DONE
1. Put on rubber gloves to protect your hands. If the hole is in the ceiling, wear safety glasses and a mask.
2. Clean out the hole by scraping with the tip of your screwdriver.
3. Brush out all remaining debris with a soft, clean paintbrush.
4. Paint the edges of the hole about 12 mm (½ in) outward with PVA bonding liquid and a paintbrush.
5. Fill the hole with joint compound using a wide putty knife.
6. Smooth the compound around the edges of the hole for the best bond. If the hole is less than 6-mm (¼-in) deep, then one application is sufficient.

7. Large, deep holes will need a second coat of compound after the first one is dry (you may have to wait 24 hours) because the compound will shrink and may even crack. Don't be alarmed! The second coat will fill in any cracks.
8. Apply PVA bonding liquid between the coats.
9. Let the plaster dry.
10. Sand, prime and paint.

Plasterboard Details

Most homes built after 1950 have walls constructed from plasterboard, which is cheaper and faster to install than new plaster walls. Plasterboard also makes for a very smooth finish that takes paint beautifully. Luckily, plasterboard is fairly simple to repair when things go wrong. Like the time you were moving a piece of furniture, and it banged right into the wall and made a dent? No problem. I have fixed a plasterboard dent after work and still had time to get ready for a date. You can, too!

The downside of plasterboard is that the sheets are very heavy, so I would not recommend installing it yourself. And forget about installing a ceiling on your own. Call in the pros for installation, but save time and money by making repairs yourself. Your walls and wallet will thank you!

DEFINING MOMENT

CORNER BEAD: This is a smaller metal or plastic strip, bent at a 90-degree angle that goes over the corner guard to protect the guard and to create a finished corner. This, along with the guard, is covered with a skim coat of joint compound to create a smooth edge.

CORNER GUARD: This is a metal edge bent at a 90-degree angle to fit over outside corners of walls. It is attached with nails, which go through ready-made holes. It helps to join plasterboard at corners. It needs to be covered with a corner bead compound to create a smooth, seamless edge.

FURRING STRIP: This is a strip of wood used to give a level surface for attaching wallboard.

PLASTERBOARD OR WALLBOARD: These are usually 1.2- x 2.4-m (4- by 8-ft) sheets made of gypsum or plaster wrapped in paper that can be nailed to wall studs to form smooth, regular walls.

POPPED NAIL: This is a plasterboard nail head that protrudes from the wall.

STUD: A post of 75 x 50 mm (3 x 2 in) or 100 x 50 mm (4 x 2 in) timber used to frame walls and partitions, they are normally placed every 400 mm (16 in) along a wall and attach to a head and sole plate. Keeping that in mind, once you have found the first stud, it is easy to locate the others by measuring.

Pop Problem Solved

REPAIR POPPED NAILS

Time: About 20 minutes, plus drying time

Popped nails are very common in new construction because the builder may have used unseasoned wood for the studs or noggings behind the plasterboard. When that unseasoned wood starts to dry out, it can shrink, causing the nail head to pop out. It's an easy problem to fix.

WHAT YOU NEED

Hammer
Plasterboard nail
Nail set
Putty knife
Joint compound
Fine sandpaper
Paint in your wall or ceiling colour
Paintbrush

· Step 3. Tap the nail just below the surface.

HOW TO GET IT DONE

1. Tap the popped nail flush to the wall with a hammer.
2. Place the point of another nail next to the nail you've just hammered. Drive it in so the head is overlapping the first nail head.
3. Using a nail set, tap the nail heads into the wall, just below the surface.
4. Use a putty knife to cover the dent made by the countersunk nails with joint compound. Be sure to smooth the compound as best you can.
5. When the joint compound is dry (2 to 24 hours, depending on weather conditions), sand it lightly until smooth. Avoid sanding the area that is not affected by the nails. The paint may come off and the paper covering might tear.
6. Apply another thin coat of joint compound over the patch.
7. Wait until that dries completely, then sand it again. Again, avoid sanding the area that is not affected by the nails.
8. Paint the area with matching colour.

Crack the Case

REPAIR SPLIT JOINT TAPE
Time: About 40 minutes, plus drying time

Joint tape is placed on all the seams where the plasterboard sheets meet. Sometimes the tape can shrink and split, usually if it's got wet and then dried. The shrinking tape will cause the joint compound covering it to crack. If you think a leak behind the wall caused the trouble, identify the origin and get it fixed; otherwise the wall will keep cracking.

WHAT YOU NEED
  Utility knife
  Putty knife
  Joint compound
  Joint tape
  Rag or sponge
  Fine sandpaper
  Primer and paint in your wall or ceiling colour
  Paintbrush

HOW TO GET IT DONE

1. Using a sharp utility knife, carefully cut out the loose tape around the split. Don't remove tape that is attached, or you may rip the paper coating the plasterboard.

2. Using a putty knife, apply a thin layer of joint compound, about 100-mm (4-in) wide, 50 mm (2 in) above and below the area.

3. Lay a strip of joint tape into the wet joint compound. Force it into the compound by pulling your putty knife over it.

4. Remove any excess compound that comes out of the sides with a damp rag or sponge.

5. Wait for the compound to dry. This could take up to 24 hours, depending on humidity conditions.

6. Use fine sandpaper to sand down the dried compound. Take care not to raise the fibres of the tape.

7. Apply another layer of compound.

8. Wait until that layer dries completely, then apply another layer of compound.

9. After the final layer of compound has dried, sand it one more time with fine sandpaper.

10. Prime and paint the area with matching wall colour.

Dent Mend

FILL IN A DENT
Time: 40 minutes, plus drying time

Dents and small holes can't be disguised with a lick of paint. You really have to fill them in if you don't want to look at them. This is especially true if you are planning to repaint your room. All the work and time you put in to give your room a fresh coat of paint will be wasted if holes are not filled in beforehand.

WHAT YOU NEED
Fine sandpaper
Putty knife
Joint compound
Primer and paint in your wall or ceiling colour
Paintbrush

HOW TO GET IT DONE
1. Lightly sand the dent and surrounding wall with fine sandpaper. Aggressive sanding will scratch the paper on the plasterboard.
2. Use your putty knife to fill the dent with joint compound.
3. When the compound is dry, sand the area down until it is smooth and flush with the wall.
4. Apply another thin layer of compound on top of the patch and let that dry thoroughly.
5. When the final coating of compound is dry, smooth the surface with fine sandpaper.
6. Prime and paint the area with matching wall colour.

Compound the Problem

PATCH SMALL TO MEDIUM HOLES IN PLASTERBOARD

Time: 60 to 90 minutes, plus drying time

Small- and medium-size holes can be filled with joint compound and covered with mesh repair tape. I had to use this technique when a friend accidentally opened a door a bit too forcefully and the glass knob created a gash in the wall.

WHAT YOU NEED

Putty knife
Joint compound
Mesh repair tape
Fine sandpaper
Primer and paint in your wall or ceiling colour
Paintbrush

HOW TO GET IT DONE

1. Using a putty knife, fill the hole with joint compound and stretch repair tape across the hole.
2. Apply two or three coats of joint compound on top of the tape. Allow drying time between each layer and sand between coats.
3. Prime and paint when the final layer is dry and sanded.

PATCH LARGE HOLES

Time: About 90 minutes, plus drying time

Large holes need to be patched with a piece of plasterboard. This takes a bit more skill than filling a dent or small hole, but it's worth the effort. Don't be afraid – you won't ruin your wall! Just take your time.

WHAT YOU NEED

Utility knife or keyhole saw
Softwood offcut for backer board
Crosscut saw
30-mm (1¼-in) plasterboard screws
Power drill with screwdriver bits
Plasterboard offcut for patching hole
Mesh repair tape
Putty knife
Joint compound
Fine sandpaper
Primer and paint in your wall or ceiling colour
Paintbrush

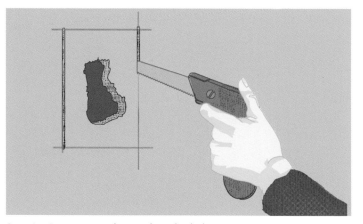

Step 1. *Cut a square larger than the hole.*

HOW TO GET IT DONE

1. Using a utility knife or keyhole saw, cut a square area larger than the hole you are patching.
2. Using a softwood offcut, cut two backer boards with a crosscut saw about 50 mm (2 in) wider than the hole.
3. Place the first backer board inside the hole and place it at the top edge of the opening. Secure it with plasterboard screws. Hold the board in place as you work. Tighten until the screw heads are below the surface.
4. Place the second backer board inside lower edge of the opening. Repeat step 3 to secure it.
5. Cut a scrap piece of plasterboard with the utility knife to fit snug in the opening. Score the board with a utility knife on one side and then break each side off until you have the desired size.
6. Screw the patch to the backer boards and tighten until the screw heads are below the surface.
7. Apply strips of mesh repair tape over all four seams.
8. Using your putty knife, cover the tape with a thin coat of joint compound. When the joint compound is dry, sand lightly with fine sandpaper.
9. Apply two more coats of joint compound, letting it dry and feathering and sanding each coat.
10. Prime and paint the patch.

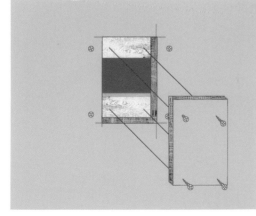

Step 6. *Screw the patch to the backer board.*

Step 8. *Cover the tape with a thin coat of joint compound.*

Mirrors, Mirrors, on the Wall

HANG PICTURES AND MIRRORS
Time: 15 to 20 minutes per picture or mirror

Photographs and artwork make a space come alive and tell visitors a story about you and your life. Family photos are too precious to tuck away in boxes. Display them so you can enjoy them everyday. I don't think my day would be very happy if pictures of my parents, my sister and especially my son didn't surround me!

Mirrors are another way to brighten up a room – literally. Mirrors reflect light and can help make long hallways or dark rooms beam. I placed a collection of mirrors down my hallway, and it doubled the amount of light in the space.

When hanging groups of pictures or mirrors, think about size, shape and frame colour. Different style frames can be unified through colour. The unifying theme of my 'hall of mirrors' is colour: all of them are white.

This simple row of mirrors in my hallway is elegant and very modern.

WHAT YOU NEED

Tape measure

Pencil

Adhesive tape

Picture hook and nail

Hammer

Level

HOW TO GET IT DONE

1. Decide where you want to put your pictures or mirrors. A basic guideline to follow is to centre the picture approximately at eye level.
2. Secure the picture hook by placing a small piece of adhesive tape on the wall below the pencil mark. This will help prevent the plaster from cracking. Now, place the nail through the picture hook and hammer it into the wall. The nail should be at a 45 degree angle to the wall.
3. Hang a picture by the wire on the back of the frame. Make any necessary adjustments so that the picture is level, using a level to check for sure.

Hanging a row of mirrors is a simple job and it's an easy way to create the illusion of light and space.

Wild for Wallpaper

Wallpaper has many great uses in different areas. But there's a good chance that you will get bored with your paper choice before it wears out. While wallpaper isn't exactly permanent, it's also not that easy to remove. It takes time and patience and can be a very messy job.

Wallpaper is also very challenging to install. Matching patterns and getting paper on straight can be nerve-racking. Many happy couples have called it quits after trying to infuse a room with country charm by hanging floor-to-ceiling plaid paper, only to wind up feeling all boxed in.

If you do have your heart set on paper, though, think about starting out small by hanging a border or perhaps papering an alcove, niche or accent wall. Small doses of pattern go a long way, and it may be all you need to create the mood you're after.

Unless you are a very experienced home decorator, I think it would be a frustrating project for you to hang your own wallpaper. I recommend hiring professional help when papering large areas. This is particularly important if you have chosen a pattern that requires precise matching skills.

DEFINING MOMENT

BOOKING: The technique of wetting and then folding the wet side of the paper in on itself to prepare it for hanging.

SINGLE ROLL: 10 m (33 ft) of wallpaper on one continuous roll.

DOUBLE ROLL: Cheaper wallpapers, such as lining and woodchip, are sometimes sold in larger rolls.

REPEAT: This is the motif on a roll of paper that is repeated over and over to create an overall pattern.

SCORING TOOL: A plastic disc or puck-shaped tool with sharp, zigzag teeth that you run across the wallpaper. This perforates the paper so that you can spray or sponge on water or a formula of fabric softener and water to soften the paste and enable you to peel the paper off the wall.

SEAM ROLLER: This is a flat rubber roller that helps remove bubbles and flattens paper at seams.

STEAMER: This is a rectangular, flat iron of sorts, generally electric, that you run across the papered wall. The heat and moist steam softens the paste and makes tearing off paper easier. You can hire steamers from local plant hire companies.

WALLPAPER PASTE OR GLUE: The glue that is used to stick paper to the wall. Most often available in premixed formulas.

If you're willing and able to pay for professional application, go to the store prepared. This means taking along fabric swatches and paint chips from the room to be papered. (This is a perfect use for your inspiration board. Take it along with you.) Shopping for patterns can be overwhelming because there are literally thousands of wallpaper patterns and hundreds of wallpaper sample books available to peruse. Give yourself a break and limit yourself to three or four books at a time. Focus on a particular style so that you can eliminate the need to look at certain categories. For example, if you are going for modern, you can automatically skip floral, fruits and representational prints (think hearts, little houses or French toile). Talk to the people in the paper department at the store and ask for help in steering you toward those manufacturers who can best fill your needs.

If you already have paper in your home and it needs repair, you can fix it without having to reinstall or remove it (unless you want to). Common paper problems are easy to solve.

Blister Bliss

FIX BLISTERS AND BUBBLES
Time: About 20 minutes

Little blisters in wallpaper are unattractive, but they can be repaired in a matter of minutes.

WHAT YOU NEED
Utility knife

HOW TO GET IT DONE
1. Cut a small X in the middle of the bubble with a utility knife.
2. Follow the directions and use the materials on page 74 for fixing torn wallpaper.

A-Peeling Fix

REPAIR PEELING OR TORN WALLPAPER

Time: About 20 minutes

Paper can peel from the top of the wall if the paper has got damp. The glue on older wallpaper can simply get old and dry out and then cause it to peel. A tear can happen for any number of reasons, most having to do with human intervention.

WHAT YOU NEED

Sponge

Wallpaper paste

Small paintbrush

Squeegee, seam roller or plastic putty knife

HOW TO GET IT DONE

1. Dampen a sponge.
2. Gently pull the torn or separated paper away from the wall to expose the underside of the paper.
3. Moisten the underside of the paper with the sponge.
4. Brush a thin, even coat of wallpaper paste on the paper with a small paintbrush.
5. Smooth the paper against the wall using a squeegee, seam roller or plastic putty knife. (A plastic putty knife is less likely to damage the paper than a metal knife.)
6. As a precaution, let the repair dry before hanging any pictures or moving furniture against the repaired wall.

Seamless Solution

STOP SEPARATING SEAMS
Time: About 30 minutes

Separating seams, like blisters, are an ugly blemish.

WHAT YOU NEED
Sponge
Wallpaper paste
Plastic putty knife
Seam roller

HOW TO GET IT DONE
1. Moisten the area where the paper has separated with a damp sponge.
2. Gently pull the loose paper away from the wall, along the separated seams.
3. Apply wallpaper paste to the underside of the paper.
4. Using a plastic putty knife, smooth the paper from the outside toward the seam on either side, placing gentle pressure on the paper to pull each side closer to the centre.
5. Finish by rolling the newly-pasted seam flat with a seam roller.

Match and Patch

PATCH A TEAR

Time: About 40 minutes, including waiting time

If your wallpaper has torn and the damaged piece cannot be salvaged or put back into place, you will have to 'match and patch' with a spare piece of paper. You may be saying to yourself that there's no way you can make an invisible patch, but it's not as difficult as it sounds. It's all in the cutting.

WHAT YOU NEED

Pencil	Sponge
Ruler	Putty knife
Extra wallpaper for patching	Paintbrush
Painter's tape	Wallpaper paste
Utility knife	Seam roller

Step 2. *Tape the wallpaper patch over the damaged area.*

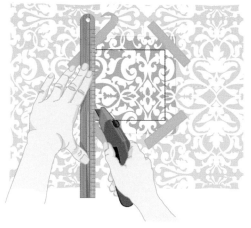

Step 3. *Cut the square shape through the patch.*

HOW TO GET IT DONE

1. Cut a piece of the extra wallpaper in a square that is 150 mm (6 in) larger than the torn area.
2. Tape the piece over the damaged area using painter's tape. (Masking tape can potentially damage the wallpaper surface further.) Be sure to match the patterns!
3. Using a utility knife and your ruler as a straightedge, with gentle pressure, cut a square or rectangle shape a little larger than the torn area through both the patch and the paper on the wall.
4. Remove the top square and put it aside. Using a damp sponge, wet the wall area where you scored. Wait 10 to 20 minutes, then gently remove the square from the wall.
5. Use a paintbrush to apply wallpaper paste to the back of the patch you cut. Apply it to the wall using a clean damp sponge and smooth out all four sides with a seam roller.

Step 4. *After wetting the damaged area, use a putty knife to remove the square of old wallpaper.*

Removing Wallpaper

At this point, you may be tired of repairing wallpaper problems and want to simply get rid of the stuff. I can't say I blame you! There are two methods for removing wallpaper. Neither is foolproof, and both require a time commitment. You can hire a steamer from a local plant hire company and steam it off. Or you can buy a scoring tool and remove it that way. It's worth investing in a scoring tool because they are made specifically for wallpaper removal. If you have a lot of wallpaper to remove, renting a steamer is the way to go. It will be a lot faster than scoring, wiping down and peeling by hand, especially if you need to remove more than one layer of wallpaper. But it's still not a fast fix. Reserve a day for this project.

Generally you do not have to score wallpaper if you are planning on using a steamer, though it is helpful if the wallpaper is particularly thick or has been painted over. I do suggest covering your floor with a canvas (not plastic) dust sheet to catch the messy paper as it peels off. I also recommend asking a friend or relative to help you. One of you can steam while the other peels off the loosened paper.

Most steamers operate in a similar fashion, but please follow the manufacturer's instructions for yours. Ask the hire firm for a demonstration. Because they want their items returned in good order, they will be more than happy to give you a lesson. Finally, remember that the steamer is hot, so use work gloves when operating and go slowly, especially in the beginning, as you get a feel for how the machine works.

The Great Rip-Off

REMOVE WALLPAPER
Time: 4 to 10 hours, depending on the size of your room

If you have a small area to deal with, such as a bathroom or one wall in a room, it may not be worth the expense of hiring a steamer. Scoring, dampening and peeling may work just as well in this instance.

WHAT YOU NEED
- Scoring tool
- Canvas dust sheet
- Bucket or paint tray
- Fabric softener
- Paint roller with a long pile or large sponge
- Rubber gloves
- Safety glasses
- Plastic putty knife

HOW TO GET IT DONE
1. Score the surface of the wallpaper with a scoring tool by running it all over the surface in a circular motion. The scoring tool will come with instructions. Read and follow them. You may be tempted to score the wall with a utility knife, but it's hard to avoid cutting through the paper and into the wall.
2. Cover the floor with a canvas dust sheet. Do not use a plastic one.
3. Fill a bucket or paint tray with a solution of 1 part water and 1 part fabric softener. There is no reason to pay extra money for wallpaper removal gels or liquids. Wallpaper paste is water-soluble and normally does not need expensive chemicals to soften it.
4. Using a paint roller or a sponge, apply the water and softener mixture very liberally to the wall. Wear rubber gloves and safety glasses because the mixture can spatter.
5. Allow the mixture to soak into the wallpaper for about 30 minutes.
6. Starting at the bottom of the wall or at a seam, gently pull away the old paper.
7. Use a plastic putty knife to remove any remaining glue and paper from the wall.
8. Once the paper and glue are completely removed, wipe down the wall with water and a clean sponge.

Preparation Is Everything

PREPARE A WALL FOR PAINTING OR NEW WALLPAPER

Time: 4 to 10 hours, depending on the size of your room and the condition of its walls

Once you have your wallpaper off, you will want to repaint the room (or maybe you want to have new paper applied). The walls need to repaired and prepared before proceeding with paint or new paper.

WHAT YOU NEED
Dust sheet
Painter's tape
Paint tray
Paint roller
Paintbrush
Interior wall paint in desired colour

HOW TO GET IT DONE
1. If the surface of the wall behind the wallpaper is damaged, you will need to repair it before painting or applying new wallpaper. See the instructions and material lists on pages 57 to 69 in this chapter for repairing plasterboard or plaster problems.
2. Prepare the room for painting by covering the floor and furnishings with a dust sheet and taping off surfaces you don't want painted with painter's tape.
3. If you are planning on re-papering the wall, paint the wall a colour that closely matches the dominant colour in your wallpaper pattern. With this step, if the seams do separate slightly (but don't come away from the wall), the seam will not show as much as it would if the wall was a contrasting colour.

A Covert Operation

PAINT OVER WALLPAPER

Time: About 8 hours, depending on the size of the room and the condition of its walls

If you want to paint a room that has been papered, it's better to remove the wallpaper first, as described on page 79. But if you simply don't have the time to remove the paper and paint the room, too, painting over paper can be a viable alternative. Just know that removing the wallpaper later will be all the more difficult because of the paint.

WHAT YOU NEED

Dust sheet

Painter's tape

Overlap adhesive

Seam roller

Paint tray and roller

Paintbrush

Fine sandpaper

Interior wall paint

HOW TO GET IT DONE

1. Prepare the room for painting by covering the floor and furnishings with a dust sheet and taping off surfaces you don't want painted with painter's tape.
2. Because you can only paint over paper that is securely pasted to the wall, inspect the paper and glue down loose edges. Refer to the instructions on page 74 for repairing wallpaper tears, peeling paper or bubbles. Seal loose seams with overlap adhesive and press the seams down securely with a seam roller.
3. Let all repairs dry before painting.
4. Apply one coat of diluted emulsion paint from a paint tray with a roller and brush to seal the surface. Let it dry. If you can still see the wallpaper pattern through the primer, apply another coat.
5. If the wallpaper seams are visible after two coats of primer, lightly file the seams smooth with fine sandpaper.
6. Apply the paint. Let it dry. Depending on the colour, you may have to apply a second coat. (Dark colours may need more than one coat to appear opaque.)

Periodically wipe the paint
buildup off the stencil using a
clean damp sponge. Don't
let the paint dry completely
on the stencil.

Fake It

PAINT A PATTERN

Time: 2 to 3 hours, depending on how complicated the stencil is

Instead of driving yourself crazy putting up wallpaper, consider stencilling your wall in a repeating pattern that looks like wallpaper. You really can achieve a truly professional custom wallpaper look using wall stencils. In fact, this technique is also a lot less expensive than wallpapering. And if you don't like it or you get bored with it, it's easy to get rid of: simply paint right over it and start again. I liked my stencilled headboard so much (see page 85) I did a tone-on-tone pattern on my bedroom's fireplace wall. Your wall stencil will come with instructions, but here are general guidelines.

WHAT YOU NEED

Emulsion paint

Emulsion glaze

Painter's tape

Pencil

Tape measure

Wall stencil

Repositional spray adhesive

Cardboard

Paint tray

Emulsion paint for stencil

High-density foam stencil roller

Paper towels

Practice board

Sponge

HOW TO GET IT DONE

1. If you want the background of your stencil to be different from your wall colour, paint it. My background was faux finished using a mixture of 50 per cent glaze and 50 per cent paint. I sponged it on over the existing wall colour. If you are painting only the centre of the wall, as I did, be sure to mark off the sides with painter's tape to create a straightedge.
2. Once the background colour was dry, I marked a level line where I wanted my stencil, using a pencil and tape measure. If you're doing the entire height of the wall, as I did, start the stencil at the top centre of the area you are stencilling.
3. Lightly spray the back of the stencil with repositionable spray stencil adhesive. This adhesive, available at any craft store or stationers, is low tack and so allows you to peel off the stencil and reposition it without

leaving any sticky adhesive on the wall. You can use the stencil four or five times before you have to re-spray. If it seems too tacky, stick it to a piece of cardboard once or twice to remove excess tack.

4. Line up two small guides cut in the stencil with the level horizontal line. Don't use the edge of the stencil as a guide. Press the stencil to the surface and mark a pencil or pin dot in the top of each of the guide holes.

Before: My bedroom was pretty dull and boring before I gave it a makeover.

5. Pour your paint into a paint tray. Paint over the stencil with the high-density foam stencil roller. This is the most important piece of equipment in this project! It will allow the paint to go on smoothly and evenly. It doesn't soak up too much paint, so it will also discourage dripping. However, be sure to blot almost all the paint on a paper towel before you put it on the wall. If you are feeling unsure, use the practice board that is included with the stencil to master the technique first.

6. When you're done with the first section, carefully peel off the stencil to the repeat position by lining up the two guide holes with the pin dots you made. Position the stencil, mark the guide holes for the next spot and paint. Continue this way until the wall or section of the wall is complete.

After: *My gorgeous new 'headboard' looks like expensive brocade wallpaper, but it's just paint.*

Opposite: *Stencilling is really easy, but the result is both professional and artistic.*

Panelling Particulars

When I hear the word 'panelling', I immediately think about basement walls or family rooms covered in dark knotty pine. Wood panelling like that was very popular in the 1970s and consequently, you may live in a home from that era and have a panelled room ... or two. Some wood panelling can be very beautiful and rich looking. For example, raised panel wainscoting is a very traditional material perfect for a den or library. And crisp white bead board panels can add texture and detail to a room where none exists. New panelling products, such as easily installed sheets of beaded MDF, have come a long way since the 1970s, making a potentially expensive proposition of adding architectural detail to a room relatively inexpensive.

But if you do have 1970s-style panelling in a room and you don't like it, there are alternatives to taking it down and dealing with what might be underneath. It's easy to make minor repairs to run-down wood walls, and a coat of paint can give old panels a completely modern look.

DEFINING MOMENT

BEAD BOARD: These sheets of MDF have grooves cut into them at regular intervals, creating the look of traditional tongue and groove panelling. Bead board panelling is thinner, lighter and much easier to install than tongue and groove. It can also be used to cover a ceiling, for example.

PANELLING: These sheets of hardboard or plywood made to look like wood are meant to cover full walls of a room. The grooves cut in the panelling are often at irregular intervals and much wider than those cut in bead board panelling. They may be attached directly to the studs in an older house.

RAISED PANELLING: These boards have bevels on all four sides of one face so that it is thicker in the centre than at its perimeter.

TONGUE AND GROOVE: These boards or planks have been finished so that there is a groove on one side of the board and a corresponding tongue on the other edge. When two pieces are placed together, the tongue of one will fit into the groove of another, forming a natural joint between the two boards. They're often used in wall cladding.

WAINSCOT: This is a wooden lining of walls often covering the lower part only of the wall. Wainscot is often done in bead board or raised panels.

Panel on the Loose

SECURE LOOSE PANELLING
Time: About 20 minutes

Sometimes panelling can buckle or start to come away from the wall, especially on timber-framed walls. The easiest way to fix a loose board is by nailing it into place. You can lever the whole sheet off and reapply panel adhesive and then put it back into place. But this may involve removing floor and ceiling moulding and trim. Because the nail fix is strong, fast and easy, I recommend it over the lever-and-glue method.

WHAT YOU NEED
Hammer
50-mm (2-in) nails
Nail set
Paint or wax touch-up stain sticks to match panelling

HOW TO GET IT DONE
1. Remove any loose nails from the loose panelling using a hammer.
2. Using the nail holes in the grooves as a guide, use fresh 50-mm (2-in) nails to nail the panelling to the wall.
3. If there are no nail holes to guide you, be sure to nail in the groove – not in the panel itself. The nails will be less visible in the grooves.
4. Stop nailing when the head is about to go into the groove space. Drive in the nail the rest of the way using a nail set.
5. Finally, touch up the nail head, if necessary, using the stain stick.

From Brown to Beautiful

. . . .

PAINT A PANELLED WALL

Time: 12 hours, including drying time

If you're tired of the rather dated panelling in one of your rooms, why not give it a coat of paint. A fresh coat of light, bright semi-gloss, satin or eggshell finish paint will instantly give old panelling a modern, clean look.

WHAT YOU NEED

White spirit
Sponges
Mask
Safety glasses
Rubber gloves
Fine sandpaper
Putty knife
Joint compound
Primer-sealer
Paint tray
Paintbrushes
Roller
Wall paint in a semi-gloss, satin or eggshell finish

HOW TO GET IT DONE

1. Wash the walls with white spirit on a sponge. This will get rid of grease and grime that will hinder painting. It will also dull any sheen the panelling may have. White spirit emits fumes, so be sure your room is well ventilated and wear a mask and safety glasses. Wear rubber gloves to protect your hands.
2. Once the walls are dry, sand down any bumps and rough spots with fine sandpaper.
3. Using your putty knife, fill any knotholes or other holes with joint compound. Once it is dry, sand spots smooth.
4. Wipe the spots with a damp sponge to remove any dust.

5. When dry, prime with primer-sealer. It gives a smooth surface a 'key' so the paint will hold. If you don't use this, the resins in knots and graining will allow them to show through. Plus, the primer-sealer eliminates the need to 'de-gloss' the wood with chemicals.
6. Once the primer is completely dry (in humid conditions, you may want to wait overnight), roll on your first coat of paint from a paint tray and cut in with a paintbrush.
7. Depending on the colour you choose, it may be necessary to give the panelling a second (and even a third) coat of paint. Wait until each coat is completely dry before judging whether you need another. If you do, paint the panelling again and wait for it to dry.

Your walls are in order – you've filled cracks, plastered holes and painted your rooms in the colours that make you happy. Next stop: floors.

Floor Show

There are so many options in flooring today; it's possible to achieve just about any kind of look from rustic to modern and everything in between. Think about it: great rooms go country with wide plank wood floors rescued from a barn, and tradition is maintained in a den or living room with the help of classic tongue and groove oak flooring. Bamboo flooring brings Asian flair to a family room. Pop the cork (flooring, that is) in kitchens or anywhere comfort underfoot is desired. Ceramic, clay or stone tile evokes a Mediterranean or tropical mood in a dining area or sunroom. Colourful carpet tiles let your imagination run rampant. And that's just the beginning. All of these ideas can be turned upside down and inside out to suit you. In short, it's a floor show and you're the star!

Choosing the right material for your floors is essential because the floor sets a room's tone. It's part of the canvas that you will fill with furnishings, rugs, accessories and your family and friends. This means a floor needs to suit both your style *and* your lifestyle. When replacing floor coverings, always keep in mind how the space will be used, how much traffic it will get and how much maintenance time you can devote to whatever material you put down, because some floors are simply more durable than others and need less upkeep. Wall-to-wall carpeting, for example, may not be practical in an entrance hall. Wood flooring is difficult to care for in a bathroom because of the dampness factor.

SAFETY NOTES

Remember to always follow the manufacturer's instructions when using any product or tool, even if it's something you've used it in the past. Manufacturers take a lot of time to write user-friendly instructions, and they know better than anyone about how to use their particular materials and tools.

Also remember when embarking on any floor or stair project to work in an area that has been cleared of debris, or any breakable or movable objects. And never place or try to balance a stepladder on stairs.

Even if you are working in a small area, protect what's around you. When working with paints or solvents of any kind, make sure the room is well ventilated. Wear a mask and safety glasses for protection against fumes and dust. Lastly, please dispose of solvents in a way that complies with local environmental rules.

Some flooring projects are do-it-yourself easy. However, installing expensive carpeting, new wood floors or heavy pieces of stone in large areas is best left to the pros. Specialized tools are needed for such projects, along with the skills to use them. But the result is always worth it: a high-quality floor of any kind, professionally installed, should last a very long time. So if you are thinking about new flooring, be assured that, chosen wisely, it's a good investment that adds value to your home. Hardwood flooring and stone or ceramic tiles, for example, are considered desirable upgrades by estate agents.

Here's more good news: if new flooring isn't part of your plans, don't worry. You can take control of the floors that you already have. Breathe new life into wooden floors by repairing minor scratches and dents or by painting over world-weary floorboards. Peel-and-stick vinyl tiles give a laundry or utility room, or even a kitchen, a fresh update in just an afternoon. I'll even show you how to tile a bathroom floor with sheets of mosaic tile using just a few basic tiling skills. It's an impressive and affordable way to turn your bathroom into a spa-like retreat.

So let's start getting underfoot!

Wood Is Good

I love the warmth and natural beauty of wood. I have wood floors throughout my house, including painted wood floors in the kitchen. Wood is so versatile: it looks right in most settings and works with every style, be it traditional, contemporary, country or urban. When properly cared for, wood can last for a very long time: two-hundred-year-old houses regularly have their original flooring in place. Hardwood flooring such as oak and maple can be sanded down and refinished many times. Softwood, like pine, is easily dented and scratched, lending a more rustic look to a room. All woods can be painted, stained and waxed, or coated with polyurethane for a hard finish that can hold up well, even in a kitchen.

When buying a wood floor, keep in mind how it will be delivered. Wood floors come as either prefinished or unfinished. An unfinished floor has to be sanded, stained and coated in your house, which can be messy and inconvenient. Prefinished floors are a bit more expensive, but they are ready to walk on as soon as they are laid.

Regardless of the type of wood flooring you choose, it should have only 7 to 10 per cent moisture content; ask about it before you buy. A floor that has too much moisture will dry differently than one with lower moisture content. Such floors will shift and separate more than floors that have been dried properly before installation.

If you already live in a home with hardwood flooring throughout, consider yourself lucky – and take good care of it.

DEFINING MOMENT

HARDWOOD: Hardwoods come from deciduous trees (those that lose their leaves in autumn). Hardwood is denser than softwood, which makes it strong enough for flooring and fine furniture. Hardwood typically used in flooring includes red and white oak, maple, mahogany, poplar, birch and walnut. Many hardwoods are very expensive to use as flooring, such as mahogany and walnut. Oak and maple are more readily available and therefore more affordable.

PLAIN SAWING: Wood is brought to mills in the form of long logs. First, the bark is removed and then it is rough-cut to prepare it for milling. One way wood is cut is by plain sawing it, which means planks are cut straight from one end of the log to the other. Wood shrinks as it dries, and plain-cut wood has a tendency to warp when dry, making it less desirable for flooring.

QUARTER-SAWN: This is wood that's cut in quarters diagonally so that each of the four pieces is at a 90-degree angle. Planks are then cut from the quarter-sawn pieces. The angle cut makes this wood much more stable and warp-resistant than plain-cut wood, making it desirable for flooring. When buying wood flooring, ask the dealer if it's quarter-sawn.

RECLAIMED WOOD: This is wood that has been rescued from barns and other old buildings. Using reclaimed wood is recycling at its best. The best way to find reclaimed wood suppliers is by searching the Internet for reclaimed wood flooring. You can also try reclamation yards. It's a specialty product, so most flooring retailers will not carry it.

SOFTWOOD: Softwoods are commonly used in the construction side of building and less often for flooring. Softwoods come from the fir family of evergreens, which includes pine. Pine is sometimes used for flooring, but it dents easily and is less versatile than hardwood flooring. Because softwoods are less expensive, they are often used for mouldings, cabinets and trim. Some common softwood varieties are pine, Douglas fir, cedar, hemlock and redwood. Cedar, pine and redwood are often used for outdoor decks, cedar and redwood because of their natural ability to resist changes in weather. Pressure-treated pine is commonly used because it's inexpensive.

TONGUE AND GROOVE: These are boards or planks of wood that are cut so that there is a groove on one side of the board and a lip or tongue on the other, making it possible to tightly lock one plank of wood to another. Most wood flooring is tongue and groove, although some reclaimed wood planking used for flooring is cut straight on the sides and is simply butted up, one against the other, and nailed into place.

WOOD LAMINATE: Wood laminates are made from several layers of wood that are bound together with glue and pressure and topped with a thin veneer of hardwood. The layers are placed so the grain direction alternates. This gives the flooring strength, durability and stability.

De-Scratch

FIX A SCRATCH
Time: About 30 minutes, plus drying time

I love rearranging my furniture, and even though I put slides on the bottom of all my large and heavy pieces, scratches are an inevitable part of redoing a room. Plus my son, Zachary, and I love to play games on the floor, and well, sometimes accidents just have a way of happening. No big deal – having fun with Zach is more important to me than any floor! In any case, most scratch accidents can be easily fixed, even if they have removed the stain from the wood. Note that you can also use this technique for matching stains on furniture.

WHAT YOU NEED
Wood stain that matches the colour of your floor
Paint stick for mixing
Fine sandpaper
White spirit
Plastic cups
Teaspoon
Artist's brushes
Varnish or polyurethane that matches the finish of your floor
Clean rags
Paper towels

HOW TO GET IT DONE
1. Select a wood stain appropriate for your floor that most closely resembles its colour. Follow the directions on the tin for preparation, which usually includes stirring gently from the bottom up with a paint stick.
2. Find an inconspicuous spot on your floor where you can perform a colour-matching test, such as under a rug or in a cupboard. Using fine sandpaper, sand down four small areas to match the level of scratch you are planning on restoring.
3. Mix the stain with white spirit in separate cups in the following ratios: straight out of the can, 4 to 1, 2 to 1, and 1 to 1. Use an old teaspoon to

measure out the quantities. One teaspoon equals one part. So, for example, the 4 to 1 ratio would be 4 teaspoons of white spirit to 1 teaspoon of stain. Stir each mixture with the spoon.

4. Apply a small amount of each mixture to a test spot using an artist's brush.

5. When all four spots are dry, apply varnish or polyurethane (whichever is used on your floor to protect it) to the test spots. This will darken them. When the finish has completely dried, you will be able to see which test matches the floor best.

6. Apply the matching mixture to the real scratch using an artist's brush. Hold the brush as close to its neck as possible. This will steady the brush and help control where the stain goes. Be careful not to get the stain anywhere but on the scratch. Blot any stray stain immediately with a rag. Let the stain dry.

7. Once the stain has dried, use a clean artist's brush to apply a coat of varnish or polyurethane. Be sure to choose a varnish or polyurethane that matches the finish already on your floor. Most finished floors are done in satin, but sometimes they can be glossier.

8. Once the first coat of varnish is dry, sand it very lightly with fine sandpaper. Wipe away any dust with a damp paper towel. Apply a second coat of varnish. Let it dry.

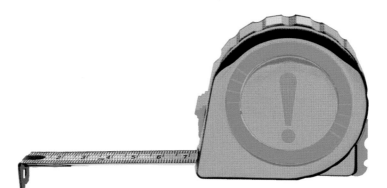

Iron Out the Problem

MEND A DENT

Time: 20 to 45 minutes, depending on the floor and the depth of the dent

A friend once had a piano moved across her wood floor, and it left a long, deep dent behind it that made her feel as if her floor was ruined forever. Not true! Because wood is a naturally resilient product, dents can be fixed with a little patience, a hot iron and some damp facecloths. She was playing a happy tune in no time.

WHAT YOU NEED

Two clean white facecloths
Steam iron
Paper towels

HOW TO GET IT DONE

1. Dampen two white facecloths (or towels) that have been washed in hot water. It's important to use extremely clean, freshly washed facecloths in this case because you want to make sure that any dyes or chemicals have been removed before using them on your floor.
2. Place the damp facecloths on the dent.
3. Set a steam iron to the cotton or hot setting. When the iron is hot, apply gentle pressure to the dent. Check it every 15 or 20 seconds to see how the dent is doing by lifting the facecloths. As one part of the dent is raised, move on to the next and so on. Dents in hardwood flooring will take longer to rise than those in softwood flooring such as pine. But the damp cloths and heat will eventually raise the dent, so be patient. Because the facecloths are thick and damp, the cotton setting will generally not burn them. However, if you do see the cloths darkening from the heat, switch to a new cloth and keep working.
4. Once the dent has been removed, pat any damp part of the floor dry with a clean paper towel.

Gouge Begone

FIX A GOUGE
Time: 15 minutes, plus 24 hours drying time

A gouge can be more disconcerting and distressing than a scratch or dent. I once dropped a heavy hammer on the floor (before I came up with a lighter, more practical one!) and – ugh – the gouge made by the claw end was pretty bad. But I knew that some wood filler would take care of the problem. The repair took some elbow grease, but it was worth it.

WHAT YOU NEED
Putty knife
Wood filler to match your stain
Fine sandpaper
Black and brown felt-tip pens
Artist's brushes
Varnish that matches the finish of your floor

HOW TO GET IT DONE
1. Use a putty knife to fill the gouge with wood filler that closely matches your floor colour. Apply it as smoothly as possible and try not to get any putty on any area other than the gouge.
2. Once the filler has dried, sand it lightly with fine sandpaper to remove any rough spots.
3. If the grain on the floor surrounding the patch is very obvious, you can simulate grain on the patch with a dark black or brown felt-tip pen. Make 'nervous' lines and then soften them quickly with a clean, dry artist's brush. If you are unsure of your artistic skills, practise with a sample putty patch placed on a scrap piece of wood.
4. Finally, varnish the area with the same finish as your floor using a clean artist's brush. Apply two coats, allowing them to dry in between.

Mind the Gap!

· ·

FIX A GAP

Time: 15 to 45 minutes, depending on number and length of gaps

Because wood is a natural product, changes in humidity levels cause it to shift, expand and contract. My house is near the ocean, which means that climate changes can really be volatile. Once in a while, I notice gaps between two floorboards. Dirt can get trapped in between these openings, and they aren't easy to clean out. Gaps look like dark lines on pickled or bleached floors. Once a gap has become permanent, it's easy to fill.

WHAT YOU NEED

Wood filler or joint compound
Putty knife
Paper towels
Fine sandpaper
Stain, varnish or polyurethane to match your floor

HOW TO GET IT DONE

1. Choose a wood filler that matches the colour of your floor. If you have pickled or bleached floors, however, white joint compound works better than wood filler.
2. Apply the wood filler or joint compound with a putty knife in the gap.
3. Wipe away any excess with paper towels.
4. Allow the material to dry completely. The filler or compound may shrink after drying. If this is the case, refill and allow the material to dry.
5. Lightly sand any rough areas with fine sandpaper.
6. If the colour of the filler doesn't match exactly, stain and varnish or polyurethane to finish.

Paint It!

. . . .

PAINT A WOOD FLOOR

Time: Up to 3 days, depending on the number of rooms you are doing and variables in drying time

There are times when refinishing an old wooden floor is impossible or impractical. Maybe it's just too expensive, or the wood is so old that it just can't take another sanding. Or you might just love the look of painted wood floors. A friend painted the floors of her little weekend cottage recently for all three reasons: it would have cost too much to bring in a professional refinisher, the floorboards were very old and worn and there was no guarantee that they would respond well to sanding – and she always wanted crisp, shiny white wooden floors. I was excited by her decision because I also knew it was a project she could do on her own. She was sceptical, but when I went through the process step-by-step, she realized it was doable and couldn't wait to get started.

My friend wanted super shiny floors, which meant she had to use high-gloss solvent-based enamel floor paint. However, if you want a softer look, you can use water-based floor paint instead. A true gleam can only be achieved with oil paint, though. So check out samples at the DIY store before you buy.

WHAT YOU NEED
    Mop
    Sandpaper
    Wood filler
    Floor primer
    Paint tray
    Paint brushes
    Roller on extension rod
    Mask
    Rubber gloves
    Floor paint

HOW TO GET IT DONE

1. Mop the floor clean.
2. Sand down any bumps or rough spots.
3. Fill any large knots, gouges and gaps with wood filler. Sand the filler smooth when dry.
4. Cover the floor with a primer made specifically for floors and allow it to dry completely. Pour the primer into a paint tray. Begin by cutting in around the perimeter of the room with a paintbrush and then fill in the middle with a roller on an extension rod.
5. When the primer has dried, which could take up to 24 hours if you are using solvent-based paint, paint the floor with your floor paint. Begin by cutting in around the perimeter of the room with a paintbrush and then fill in the middle with a roller.
6. Once the first coat of floor paint has dried completely (up to one day), check for any imperfections or obvious bumps or paint drops or blobs (it happens!). Sand them down with medium grit sandpaper and wipe away any dust with a very slightly damp cloth, then give the floor a second coat. If you are going over a very dark floor with a light paint, or a light floor with a dark paint, you may have to give the floor a third coat. If that's the case, wait for the second coat to dry completely before painting with a third coat. It's best to wait 24 hours before moving furniture back in to make sure the floor is completely dry.

Note: Don't paint yourself into a corner! Move towards an exit!

SAFETY NOTES

If you use solvent-based enamel paint, you must work in a well-ventilated room and wear a mask and rubber gloves.

The Great Pretenders: Vinyl and Laminates

I remember the vinyl floor in my childhood kitchen. It was easy to keep clean and practical, which was a good thing for my mother, considering that my sister, Caryn, and I were two very active girls. Vinyl, whether in sheets or tiles, can stand up to a busy family's lifestyle. It's quiet underfoot, water-resistant, inexpensive and available in lots of colours and patterns. But it doesn't last as long as other flooring, and repairs on vinyl, while very doable, tend not to be as invisible as repairs on other materials.

Peel-and-stick tiles make do-it-yourself projects possible. They offer a quick solution to recovering the floor of a small bathroom or kitchen, and the results buy you some time while you save for sturdier flooring.

Vinyl can be printed with almost any pattern, emulating wood, stone or brick. In the case of linoleum-like vinyl products, it can just be itself – a synthetic square in any range of colours and textures.

Laminates, on the other hand, take faux finishes one step further. Laminates have a dense fibreboard core with a paper pattern layer sealed under high-pressure with a resin coating. That paper layer is usually a high-quality photograph of wood or stone. The best laminates can be very deceiving; they really can look like whatever they are pretending to be. Laminates are sold as planks and panels. Installation of laminates is different from other types of flooring material in that the planks are attached to each other and not to the floor itself. A vapour barrier, usually a sheet of plastic or foam, sits between the floor and the laminate planks, creating a 'floating' system. Some laminate floating floors now come in a clicking system and don't require any glue. Instead of being glued together, the planks work on a tongue and groove system which fits together tightly and requires only minimal trimming with a utility knife to fit around corners. That means you can put a floating floor in yourself. Start small: try a click-system laminate floor in a small room first.

Laminates have a lot going for them. They are virtually stainproof and fade-resistant, easy to clean, affordable and comfortable to stand on for long periods. They can be susceptible to damage from excess moisture, so they are not the best bet in a family bathroom.

A Square Deal

REPLACE A VINYL TILE
Time: About 30 minutes

Replacing a damaged vinyl tile is even easier than patching a sheet of vinyl floor. Because the entire tile can be replaced, the 'patch' will be invisible!

WHAT YOU NEED
- Hair dryer
- Putty knife
- Vacuum
- Vinyl adhesive
- Notched trowel
- Extra tile
- Sponge
- Rolling pin

HOW TO GET IT DONE
1. Use a hair dryer to heat the damaged tile. This will soften the adhesive and make it easy for you to lever it up.
2. After levering up the tile, use a putty knife to scrape away the old adhesive. Use the hair dryer to soften any remaining adhesive. Vacuum the area to get every scrap up. You want the area to be as clean and smooth as possible.
3. Apply vinyl adhesive to the floor with a notched trowel.
4. Press the tile in place. Start at the centre and work toward the edges to get out all the air bubbles.
5. Wipe any excess adhesive off the edges with a damp sponge.
6. Roll the patch with a rolling pin. Wipe the edges one more time to remove any excess adhesive.
7. Let the adhesive dry well before walking on the new tile.

Patch Things Up

PATCH A VINYL FLOOR
Time: About 40 minutes

I recently received a letter from a woman who said the vinyl floor in her kitchen tore after her husband dragged a cooker across it. She had been staring at the damage for more than a month. Clearly, no one was planning on repairing it, so she decided to give it a go herself and wrote to me for advice. This is the kind of letter I love because it gives me a chance to share exactly how to fix the tear and support her can-do attitude at the same time. Once the woman had got the rush that fixing her floor gave her, she was ready to conquer the world!

A successful patch in sheet vinyl can be made only if you have extra flooring on hand. Luckily, my pen pal had extra flooring in her garage. Most of the time, when you have sheet flooring installed, the installer will leave what's left behind. Don't throw it away. It's worth hanging onto in case you have to make a patch. The patch will not be invisible, but it's better than having a wounded floor.

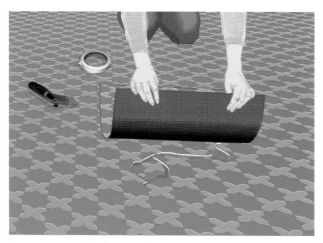

Step 2. *Cover the damaged area with the patching material, lining up the pattern.*

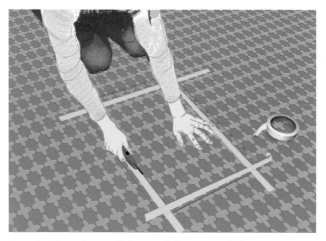

Step 4. *Once the patch is taped down, carefully cut through both layers.*

WHAT YOU NEED

Sharp straightedge utility knife
Extra piece of vinyl flooring
Masking or duct tape
Hair dryer
Putty knife

Vacuum cleaner
Vinyl adhesive
Notched trowel
Sponge
Rolling pin

HOW TO DO IT

1. Using a sharp straightedge utility knife, cut a piece of new vinyl flooring that is larger than the damaged area.
2. Cover the damaged area and line up the pattern of the patch with the pattern on the floor.
3. Tape the replacement piece over the damaged area with masking or duct tape to secure it in place.
4. Use the utility knife to cut through both layers of vinyl. Cut an area just larger than the damaged area so the hole and the patch will be exactly the same size.
5. Take the tape off and put the patch aside. Use a hair dryer to heat the damaged vinyl. This will soften the adhesive and make it easy for you to lever it up.
6. Use a putty knife to scrape away the old adhesive. Use the hair dryer to soften any remaining adhesive. Vacuum the area to get every scrap up. You want the area to be as clean and smooth as possible.
7. Apply vinyl adhesive to the floor with a notched trowel.
8. Press the patch in place. Start at the centre and work toward the edges to get all the air bubbles out.
9. Wipe any excess adhesive off the edges with a damp sponge.
10. Roll over the patch with a rolling pin using your full body weight. Wipe the edges one more time to remove any excess adhesive.
11. Let the adhesive dry well before walking on the patch.

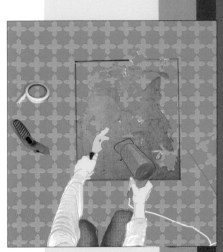

Step 6. *Use a hair dryer to soften the adhesive.*

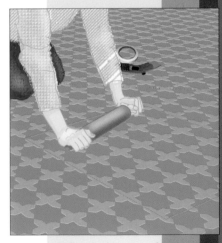

Step 10. *Roll over the area of the patch.*

The Hard Stuff: Ceramic, Stone and Porcelain

Stone and tile installation can seem pretty intimidating. It's true that creating a floor with heavy pieces of slate or marble might be best left to the pros, especially if you're just starting out on home improvement projects. But there are tiling projects that are within reach, such as replacing an old vinyl floor with tile. You'll get a professional, designer look with just a few basic skills!

For example, I recently added a bathroom to my home. While I certainly didn't do the complicated plumbing work myself, or the installation of the heavy shower tray, I did do several smaller jobs, including putting in a new tap (you'll read how in Chapter 5) and tiling the floor with a beautiful glass mosaic squares. The 25-mm (1-in) squares come on 300-mm (12-in) mesh sheets, which are easy to trim to size.

All floor-tiling projects should start with a clean slate. In my case, the bathroom floor was concrete: there was no old flooring to remove, so I

DEFINING MOMENT

CERAMIC TILE: For this type of tile, a mixture of clays are pressed into shape and fired at high temperatures. The bisque, or body, of the tile may then be glazed or left unglazed.

GLAZED TILE: A glazed tile has a coating that is fired on after the tile has been fired once. It seals the tile (making it less prone to staining) and can give it a variety of finishes, from matt to high gloss.

GROUT: This thin mortar is used to fill joints between tiles.

PORCELAIN TILE: This is a type of tile made from a blend of fine-grain clays and other minerals to produce a very dense, hard product that is water and stain resistant. Porcelain tile will withstand years of heavy foot traffic both indoors and out and still look good.

THIN-BED ADHESIVE: This is the adhesive that you use to hold tiles in place. It's available ready-mixed or as a powder you mix with water.

UNGLAZED TILE: Unglazed tile has no surface coating. The colour is the same on the face of the tile as it is on the back, resulting in very durable tiles that do not show the effects of heavy traffic. The most common unglazed tiles are red quarry tiles.

THE LOWDOWN ON THIN-BED ADHESIVE

This is the mortar adhesive that holds the tile in place. Manufacturers recommend different ways of mixing and using their products, so please follow directions provided by the maker for the specific brand you buy. Here are some general tips to keep your tiling on track.

- Use grey adhesive if you plan to use grey or darker coloured grout. Use white adhesive for light coloured grout. Grout seals the seams and gives the floor a finished look. You can use the adhesive as grout, or you can use a mortar product specifically designated as grout.

- Multipurpose and polymer-modified adhesives can be used for installing most ceramic tiles. Porcelain tiles benefit by being installed with latex-modified adhesive.

- Mix only a small amount of adhesive at a time until you become used to its setting time, which will vary according to temperature and humidity.

- Allow at least 16 hours – ideally 24 hours – for the tile to set before walking on it.

could get down to business pretty quickly. The WC had yet to be installed, too. If you are replacing a floor in an existing bathroom, you must hire a plumber to remove the WC first, then replace it when you are finished with the tiling job.

If you are replacing the vinyl in your bathroom, the old flooring has to come up. If you are removing sheet vinyl, use a sharp utility knife to cut around the perimeter of the room. Then cut the floor into four sections. Lever up a corner of each section and pull! You can do it. If it's stuck, use a hair dryer or heat gun to soften the adhesive backing. If you're removing vinyl tiles, lever them up with a putty knife and use the hair dryer to soften the glue. Scrape as much adhesive off the floor as you can, then vacuum.

A floor scraper, which has a wide blade attached to a long pole, gives you the leverage and sharpness you need to scrape up stubborn adhesive. Eventually, you'll have a vinyl-free floor. Ceramic or stone tile is thicker than vinyl so the threshold strips between rooms may have to be removed and replaced when you are finished the job.

Applying Style

TILE A BATHROOM FLOOR WITH MOSAIC SHEET TILES
Time: 4 to 8 hours, plus drying time

Tiling is something that you may think is reserved for the pros. But if you read through these instructions carefully, gather all the materials together before you begin, and then go through this project step-by-step, you can do it. The secret is the mosaic sheets, which makes tile cutting virtually unnecessary. If you are hesitant to try the project for the very first time on your very well-used bathroom floor, how about a less-conspicuous utility room? The process is exactly the same.

WHAT YOU NEED

Prybar or crowbar

Safety glasses

9-mm (³⁄₈-in) exterior-grade plywood (if the subfloor is wood)

25-mm (1-in) deck screws (if the subfloor is wood)

Utility knife

Thin-bed adhesive

Chisel

Tape measure

Pencil or chalk line

Floor tiles in sheets (be sure to buy 10 per cent more than you need; your supplier will help you calculate how much you need to buy)

Bucket for mixing adhesive

Notched trowel

Plastic spacers

Large sponges

Tile grout

Grout float

Paper towels

HOW TO GET IT DONE

1. If you are tiling an existing bathroom, you must remove the WC first. You can hire a plumber to remove and replace it.
2. You may also have to remove skirting boards from the room. Using a prybar or crowbar, gently lever off the pieces without breaking them so you can reinstall them when you're done. Remove all nails from the wood and use new nails when reinstalling.
3. Wear safety glasses at all times. Prepare the floor by cleaning it. If the subfloor is wood, lay plywood over the subfloor with deck screws every 200 mm (8 in). Deck screws are galvanized to protect them from rust, so

they are important to use in this job. If you are applying the tiles to a concrete floor, fill in any cracks or hollows with tile adhesive. Chisel away any raised areas.

4. With a tape measure, find and mark the centre of the room. Measure from the middle of the walls, front to back and side to side and mark each line with a pencil or chalk. When measuring, take cabinets and other permanently covered areas of the floor into consideration. The point at which the two lines meet in the centre of the floor is your centre mark.

5. Lay out the tiles in a dry run to see if you like the way they look and to see where you may need to cut the mesh backing. While it's impossible to determine what the final cuts will be, you can get a rough idea of where the tile sheets will need to be trimmed. Start at the centre mark and work outward toward the walls.

6. Once you have found the arrangement you like, take up the tiles and prepare enough adhesive in a bucket to cover about a quarter of the room. The adhesive should be the consistency of peanut butter.

7. Trowel the adhesive directly onto the floor with a notched trowel, pulling it toward you in an arc. This enables you to pick up any waste more easily and put it back into the bucket.

Step 7. *Trowel adhesive onto the floor in an arc.*

Step 8. *Place tile sheets directly on the adhesive, but don't press down the tile too forcefully.*

8. Carefully place the mosaic sheet on the adhesive. Be particularly careful not to press too hard as this will squeeze the adhesive out to the sides. Twist the tiles slightly into place. Set plastic spacers next to each tile to keep the tile rows evenly spaced. Place tiles on either side and then complete the next row until a quarter of the room is complete.

9. Wipe away any excess adhesive with a barely damp sponge. Rinse the sponge.

10. Repeat steps 7 to 9 until the room is completely tiled. Using a clean sponge, wipe away as much excess adhesive from the top of the tiles as you can.

11. Let the adhesive set overnight.

12. Mix the grout to the consistency of cake mix. It should be looser than the adhesive. Apply the grout with the grout float, moving across the tile on the diagonal and pulling it toward you. Use light pressure to push the grout in between the tiles. Use the float to take away excess grout.

13. Wait about 20 minutes, before the grout is completely set, and wipe away as much excess grout as you can with a damp sponge. There should be as little grout on top of the tiles as possible. It is next to impossible to remove it once it dries.

14. Allow the grout to dry. The next day, polish off the grout 'haze' from on top of the tiles with a paper towel.

Step 12. Apply the grout.

Tiling a floor is within your reach. And the beauty and value it adds to your home makes learning tiling skills worth your while.

If It's Broken, Fix It

REPLACE A BROKEN TILE
Time: About 45 minutes

I have a girlfriend who loves to cook. When she gets going with pots and pans, watch out! She can really make a mess, but the end result is delicious. One evening she called me in tears. 'Barbara, I have to replace my entire kitchen floor!' she cried. I gently asked her to slow down and tell me what had happened. In her haste, she had dropped a cast iron pot on her beautiful tile floor, and one of the tiles cracked. I'm not a gourmet like my friend, but I do love my kitchen, so I could definitely relate to my friend's distress: it's a drag when something you love gets damaged. But I reassured her that there is no reason to replace an entire tile floor if one or even four tiles have been cracked or broken. Removing a damaged tile and laying a new one is a straightforward do-it-yourself project, even for clumsy cooks!

WHAT YOU NEED

Hammer

Grout saw or a rotary tool with a cutting tip

Safety glasses

Hand towel

Work gloves

Cold chisel

Vacuum cleaner

Matching replacement tile

Crayon (if you need to cut the replacement tile)

Manual tile cutter (if you need to cut the replacement tile)

Tile adhesive (for this job, you can use premixed adhesive)

Putty knife

Notched trowel

Grout to match what's already on the floor

Grout float

Sponge

HOW TO GET IT DONE

1. Isolate the damaged tile or tiles so that other tiles don't get damaged in the process. (It's likely that you'll have to break up the cracked or damaged tile with a hammer in order to get it out.) To protect the surrounding tiles from your hammer's shock waves, remove the grout that surrounds it with a grout saw. A grout saw is very inexpensive and

easily found at any DIY store. Simply drag the saw blade through the grout. It will take some time to cut all the way through (up to 20 minutes), but it's time well spent. You could also use a rotary tool with a cutting tip to take out the grout, but unless you already have one, a grout saw is cheaper and just as good. If you do use a rotary tool, use safety glasses.

2. Once you've removed all the grout around the damaged tile, lay a hand towel over the tile and hit it with a hammer until the tile is broken into pieces. Put on your work gloves and remove the pieces. Discard them.

3. Use a cold chisel to remove the adhesive from the floor. Take care not to gouge the floor surface. Wear safety glasses to protect your eyes from any flying debris.

4. Vacuum up any small rubble. If the floor's not completely clean, the replacement tile won't adhere properly.

5. You should have one full box of extra tiles on hand (for just this sort of occasion) but if you don't, you can buy a new one. If you can't find an exact match, try to find one that closely resembles it. A slightly mismatched tile is better than a broken one.

6. If you are replacing a tile that has been cut to fit a space, measure it by taking the replacement tile and placing it on top of the area where the old tile was removed. Line up the edges by matching the tile pattern, if there is one, and use a crayon to mark the cut line. Use a manual tile cutter to make the single, firm cut along the line you made. You can then snap the tile along the line.

7. In this situation, it's better to use premixed tile adhesive for the back of the new tile than trying to trowel adhesive onto the floor. Use a putty knife to 'butter' the back of the tile with adhesive. Create even notches in the adhesive with the notched trowel.

8. Place the tile in the space and tap it down gently with a hammer covered with the towel, or even better a rubber mallet. Be gentle; you don't want to break another tile! Make sure it is level with the other tiles.

9. Let it dry for 24 hours before applying grout.

10. Use a grout float to press the grout around the edges of the tile. Use a sponge to wipe the excess from the top of the tile. After about 30 minutes, wipe away any grout that has formed on the tile with a damp sponge. Wait another day before walking on it.

Carpet Comfort

An uncovered wooden staircase can be noisy when used; carpeting helps muffle sounds underfoot.

Carpet can make a room feel cosy and warm. There's nothing like it in a bedroom. Carpet is great in children's and babies' rooms, too. It offers just enough cushioning for a little one taking his or her first steps. In a living room, the right carpet can add to an elegant, formal atmosphere. Carpet also muffles noise, which makes it great for staircases and hallways or other heavily trafficked areas. And of all the options in floor covering, carpet is one of the most affordable.

If you're thinking of replacing the carpet in your living or family room, or adding it to a nursery or bedroom, it's worth taking some time to understand the choices. Just because a carpet is expensive doesn't mean it's 'the best' or right for you. There is so much variation in carpet prices. Synthetic carpet is inexpensive, but wool or silk wall-to-wall can sometimes cost more than putting down hardwood floors. It's best to be informed before you buy.

Wool carpet is considered a luxury product because it's so expensive. Because it's so durable, stain resistant, and easy to clean, wool lasts longer than synthetic fibres, and so in the long run, it can be a very practical choice. Wool is a great choice for heavily trafficked areas such as stairs and hallways. I recently covered the stairway in my home with a wool 'sisal' runner. Real sisal, which is also a natural product, cannot be cleaned, and so it's not practical for busy families.

Nylon carpet is also quite durable and does a pretty good job of imitating wool's appearance and comfort underfoot. It is also fairly stain resistant and easy to clean.

Polypropylene is strong, and water- and stain-resistant, making it a good choice for Berber-style carpet. It's not as resilient as nylon, but it's a good price. If you use polypropylene, check with the dealer to make sure it has been treated with fire retardant, because it is flammable if left untreated.

Carpet tiles are a great choice for do-it-yourself carpeting projects. You cannot install them over existing carpeting, but they can be easily placed over any other flat surface: a plywood subfloor, vinyl tile, wood, and even concrete. Several manufacturers offer carpet tiles in a range of colours and textures, so you are not limited as far as creating a look. Best of all, carpet tiles can be pulled up and taken with you to a new house or apartment.

Wool is a sturdy, beautiful choice for well-travelled areas in your home, such as stairs. This wool runner looks like sisal, but it's a lot stronger, softer under foot and easier to clean.

Most stick to the floor with little adhesive pads that allow the tiles to be moved around and rearranged. The biggest advantage carpet tiles offer is spot replacement. If a serious accident occurs (think sick puppy or spilled grape juice), you can simply pick up a tile and replace it with a new one.

Whatever kind of carpet you decide to buy, remember that regular maintenance will prolong its life and impart a good-as-new appearance. Follow the manufacturer's recommended cleaning methods. Vacuum regularly – at least twice a week – to remove loose fluff and dust. Vacuuming will never hurt your carpet if done properly because it ensures dirt doesn't get embedded in the carpet and ruin the fibres. Have a professional deep-clean your carpet once a year.

DEFINING MOMENT

BERBER: Loop-pile carpet tufted with thick yarn, such as wool, berber is comfortable to walk on and creates a modern, informal look. Berber is now used loosely to describe sculptured carpeting.

BINDING: This is a band of fabric sewn over a carpet edge to protect, strengthen or decorate it.

BROADLOOM: This is carpet produced in widths wider than 2 m (6 ft). Standard broadloom is usually about 4 m (13 ft) wide.

DENSITY: The density is the amount of pile yarn in the carpet and the closeness of the tufts. In general, the denser the pile, the better the performance.

HAND: This term is used to describe how carpeting feels when you run your hand over it: smooth, textured, velvety and so on.

PILE: This is the surface of carpet, also called the face or nap.

PLUSH: A smooth-textured carpet in which individual tufts are only minimally visible and the overall visual effect is that of a single level of yarn ends – is sometimes called 'velvet-plush'.

PLY: Here single carpet yarn ends have been ply-twisted together to form a plied yarn, e.g. two-ply or three-ply.

SAXONY: In this cut-pile carpet texture with twisted yarns in a relatively dense, erect configuration, the effect is well-defined tuft tips.

SISAL: Originally made of vegetable fibres, carpet has recently attained the look of natural sisal with softer synthetic alternatives. Wool and synthetic alternatives are almost worry-free and offer a variety of interesting textures, patterns and prints.

TILES: A relatively new product, carpet tiles usually come with the carpet pad attached and ready to install. Carpet tiles are made in a variety of patterns and textures, including shag and Berber styles.

TUFTED: Most broadloom carpeting is tufted. Continuous strands of yarn are stitched into a primary backing. A latex coating locks the loops in place. Then a secondary backing is applied for strength and durability.

Out, Damned Spot!

Most carpet available today is stain-resistant (but not stainproof), which means that many (but not all) spills can be removed … if you act fast. The longer you wait to take care of an accident, the greater the chance that it will become a permanent part of your carpet. Check with the carpet manufacturer for their specific recommendations. Here are some easy, old-fashioned ways I use to deal with common stains using ingredients you probably already have on hand. I'm not sure who came up with these ideas, but I remember my mother using these techniques to deal with carpet mishaps. Remember to always pretest any solvent in an inconspicuous area before you use it on the actual stain.

INK

Solvent: rubbing alcohol Apply rubbing alcohol to a clean white cloth, white paper towel or cotton ball. If the spot extends deep into the pile, use a blotting motion until the spot is removed or no colour is transferred to the cloth. Do not allow the alcohol to penetrate into the backing because this will destroy the latex bond. If the spot is on the surface only, rub in one direction at a time. Never use a circular motion to remove a spot because this may destroy the texture. Stop if the spot is removed. If not, go to the next step.

Apply a small quantity of detergent solution to the spot. To make the detergent solution, mix ¼ teaspoon of a hand-dishwashing detergent that does not contain lanolin or bleach with 1 litre of water. Use a blotting motion to work the detergent into the affected area. If the spot is being removed, continue applying detergent and blotting with a white paper towel until the spot is removed.

Rinse with tap water using a spray bottle, and blot to remove excess moisture.

Spray lightly with water, do not blot this time; apply a pad of paper towels and allow the area to dry.

If there is still some stain on the carpet, moisten the tufts in the stained area with 3 per cent hydrogen peroxide. Let it stand for an hour. Blot and repeat until the carpet is stain free. Light causes peroxide to change back to water so no rinsing is necessary.

CARING FOR YOUR VACUUM CLEANER

With these simple steps in mind, your vacuum cleaner should serve you well for many years.

- Follow the vacuum cleaner manufacturer's instructions.
- Change the vacuum bag when it becomes more than half full. As the bag becomes full, efficiency is reduced.
- Keep the vacuum brushes and hoses clean and free of debris.
- Inspect belts to make certain they are working properly.
- Always keep a spare belt for replacement.

RED WINE

Solvent: equal parts dishwashing liquid and hydrogen peroxide Spray or dab the mixture on the stain. Blot with a paper towel. Because peroxide is a bleaching agent, the remedy could potentially bleach some coloured rugs. Always test a small inconspicuous patch before using it on the stained area.

WAX

Solvent: denatured alcohol First, scrape away as much wax as you can. Then place a sheet of blotting paper, or a portion of a brown paper bag on top of the wax. Press the tip of a warm iron gently over the affected area until the wax melts and is absorbed by the paper. Lift the paper from the carpet. Dab a small amount of denatured alcohol onto the stain if any candle dye is left on the carpet. Rinse with water.

Fire the Damage

FIX A BURN

Time: About 45 minutes, not including tape setting time

If the burn is small and on the very top or surface of the carpet, you can improve the situation by carefully clipping off blackened ends of tufts with small, sharp scissors. Trim the surrounding tufts to minimize indentation.

If the burn is more severe and has penetrated the carpet, you will have to remove and patch the section with a spare piece of carpet. You can remove a piece from a cupboard or other inconspicuous place or use extra you may have saved. This technique can also be used for those stubborn stains that resist removal.

WHAT YOU NEED

Spare carpet
Sharp utility knife
Tape measure
Work gloves
Vacuum cleaner
Double-sided carpet tape
Books

HOW TO GET IT DONE

1. Using a sharp utility knife, cut a patch of spare carpet into a square or rectangle, about 2.5 cm (1 in) bigger than the size of the burn.
2. Put on work gloves and, using the utility knife, cut out a patch round the burnt area the same size as the patch with the utility knife.
3. Vacuum the area.
4. Stick double-sided carpet tape to the back of the carpet to frame the hole. Press the patch into place and weight it overnight with a pile of books.
5. Vacuum it again to blend the seams.

Your floors are fixed, and you did it yourself. Let's roll out the welcome mat and see just how much you can do to repair, enhance and improve your windows and doors. Quite a bit, actually!

Windows (and Doors) of Opportunity

Natural light and fresh air are so important to me. I love to feel and see the sun streaming in through my bedroom windows in the morning. My son, Zachary, and I often watch how the sky changes as the sun sets, and these are moments I treasure. Cool breezes on a summer evening brings out my romantic side, and listening to rain drops as they hit my windowpanes is both calming and meditative. These are just a few reasons why windows and doors are so important to me.

Windows and doors are also integral parts of a home's structure. They play an important role in controlling light, ventilation and temperature. Windows and doors can also be architecturally beautiful as well as functional. If you're upgrading windows, choose a style that matches your needs both practically and stylistically. For example, casement windows scream modern, while double-hung sash windows with 12 panes over 12 panes say traditional. The wrong windows can make a house look awkward or off balance, but properly chosen windows beautifully placed can make even the simplest house 'best of class'. Windows should be placed to create balance and harmony on the exterior of a house, as well as to take advantage of the best views and bring light into the home.

SAFETY NOTES

Remember always to follow the manufacturer's instructions when using any product or tool, even if you've used it in the past. Manufacturers take a lot of time to write user-friendly instructions, and they know better than anyone about how to use their particular material or tool. Also remember when embarking on any window or door project to work in an area that has been cleared of debris or any breakable or movable objects. When you are working with saws or other power tools, wear safety glasses and gloves. Follow product instructions. When working with paints or solvents of any kind, make sure the room is well ventilated. Wear a mask and safety glasses for protection against fumes and dust. Please dispose of solvents in a way that complies with local environmental rules.

Exterior doors should be sturdy and well made, with good quality, attractive locks strong enough to keep intruders out, while offering style and substance inside. Exterior doors can be solid or windowed, simply chic or lavishly ornate. Either way, they should fit in with the style of your home and welcome guests.

Like doors to the outside, interior doors should be strong, close properly, and blend well with the style and décor in your home. If you don't love the doors inside your house, you can change them without replacing them. The simplest hollow core, solid core or veneer doors can be transformed with paint, by adding moulding and decorative trim, or by changing knobs and other hardware.

Maintenance is essential when it comes to doors and windows. Sticky windows and wobbly doorknobs are annoying to deal with and potentially dangerous. Simple repairs and upgrades can make a big difference in your home and in your ability to tackle other, more challenging projects.

Choosing and caring for doors and windows is an open-and-shut case, so let's get started.

Winning Windows

Like human eyes, which have been called the windows to the soul, windows are your home's eyes. In short, the type of windows you use will say a lot about the design of your home. Here's a look at some common styles.

Bay windows are often multi-paned, but they don't have to be. They can make a room feel larger without expensive structural changes because they stick out beyond the walls, and they are usually supported by brackets on the outside of the house.

Casement windows (see opposite) pivot out on hinges mounted on the side, and are secured by a crank handle. They are available in many sizes and give a house a contemporary look. They allow unobstructed views and good ventilation.

Double-hung sash windows slide up and down and are found on many traditional-style houses. Variations include 6 over 6 and 4 over 4, which means the top and bottom each have either 6 panes or 4 panes, separated by glazing beads.

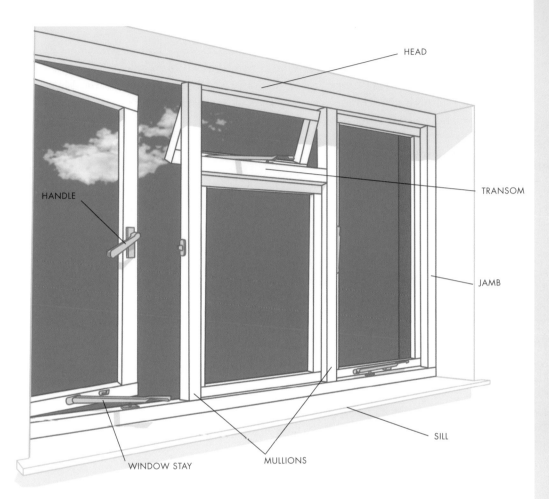

HEAD

TRANSOM

HANDLE

JAMB

WINDOW STAY

MULLIONS

SILL

Palladian windows have an arched or rounded top. They are often decorative and cannot be opened.

Sliding windows are like small sliding glass doors. They operate the same way and offer a panoramic view. They have two sides, but only one side slides open.

Skylights are installed in the roof and introduce extra light and ventilation without taking up wall space.

Top hung windows pivot out on hinges mounted at the top. They provide ventilation without letting in moisture.

The type of glass used in windows also has to be considered. Single-pane glass is suitable only in very mild climates. In warmer climates, double-glazed tinted glass reduces heat buildup. Sealed unit double glazing has a sealed air space between the layers of glass that helps reduce heat loss. Safety glass provides extra strength and is used in patio and sliding glass doors and large picture windows.

DEFINING MOMENT

ALUMINIUM: No longer widely used, but common as replacement windows installed during the 1960s and 1970s. Older windows were usually single-glazed and suffered from being very good conductors of heat, causing condensation to form on the frames as well as on the glass in cold weather. Newer types were double-glazed for extra warmth, and the frames incorporated plastic thermal breaks to eliminate the condensation problem. The bare metal tends to oxidize over time, forming an unsightly white coating, but frames can be painted to obliterate this.

HARDWOOD: The best wooden windows are made from a variety of durable hardwoods, and are intended to be stained or varnished rather than painted to show off the wood grain. High-performance versions incorporate draughtproofing round all opening casements and vents, and are invariably fitted with sealed-unit double glazing. They are available in a range of casement and sliding sash styles.

PLASTIC: Many new homes are now fitted with windows made from a plastic material called unplasticised polyvinyl chloride (uPVC for short). The extrusions used to make up the frames are reinforced with a steel core for strength and security, and are made in white and a variety of simulated wood finishes. The frames are supplied complete with sealed-unit double glazing, and also have built-in security locks. Most modern replacement windows are now made from uPVC.

SOFTWOOD: Softwood windows are cheaper than other types, but are not as durable unless they are well maintained. They are available in a wide range of standard sizes, in both casement and sash styles, and are usually supplied factory-primed ready for staining or painting. The frames can take single or double glazing.

First Glass

REPLACE A BROKEN WINDOWPANE
Time: About 1 hour

When one of Zachary's friends hit a baseball through one of my windows, I had to replace it. I think Zach was more upset than I was!

WHAT YOU NEED

Work gloves

Safety glasses

Cold chisel

Hammer

Pliers

Tape measure

New glass

Glazing sprigs

Glazing putty

Putty or glazing knife

Paint

Paintbrush

HOW TO GET IT DONE

1. Put on your work gloves and safety glasses. Lift out as much of the broken glass as you can. Loosen any remaining pieces still held fast in the putty by tapping them with a hammer. Wrap up the glass in newspaper, then in a bag, and put it in the dustbin.

2. Use the chisel to chip out all the old, hard putty from the rebate – the L-shaped recess in which the glass sits. You are likely to find some small headless nails (called glazing sprigs) buried in the putty; they held the original pane in position when it was installed. Prise them out with pliers and throw them away.

3. Measure up for the new pane. Take height measurements at each side of the rebate, and width measurements at the top and bottom. If the measurements of either dimension differ slightly, note the smaller ones in each case. Subtract 3 mm ($\frac{1}{8}$ in) from each measurement to allow for clearance all round. Visit your local glass merchant and order the new pane, plus enough putty to bed it in. If the old glass was patterned, take a piece with you so the glass merchant can try to supply a good match.

4. Scoop some putty out of the container and knead it in your hands to make it soft and pliable. Then press in a bed of putty all round the rebate with your putty knife.

5. Rest the bottom edge of the pane in the rebate, stand it upright and push it gently into the bedding putty. Then press each edge in more firmly to compress the putty – you will see it squeezing out on the inside of the glass. Do not press the centre of the pane or you may crack it. Trim off excess bedding putty from the inside of the window.

6. Tap in new glazing sprigs at roughly 150 mm (6 in) intervals all round the pane so they press against it and hold it in place. Let the hammer slide across the surface of the glass so the sprigs go in straight.

7. Knead some more putty into a sausage shape and press it into the angle between the glass and the edge of the rebate. When you have applied this facing putty all round the pane, draw the flat edge of your putty knife along it to smooth it to an angle of about 45 degrees, level with the bedding putty on the inside.

8. Seal the putty to the glass by drawing a dry paintbrush along the junction. Be sure to leave the putty to harden for at least 14 days before painting over it.

Full Window Fashion

Window treatments such as drapes, curtains, sheers and swags can make a dramatic difference in the way your rooms look with very little effort on your part. Tired of looking at the brick wall facing your kitchen window, or worse, your neighbour's dustbins? Simple café curtains clipped to tension rods take just minutes to make and instantly hide unpleasant or uninspiring views.

Hanging curtain rods takes a bit more planning, but still, in less than 45 minutes, you'll be on your way to transforming a dull family room into a dramatic backdrop for your favourite soirées. And curtains don't have to be expensive. Let your imagination run wild: inexpensive Indian bedspreads, sari fabric, vintage materials and even sheets can be repurposed into drapes and curtains. Ready-made curtains can be altered for a custom look. I did that, and it not only resulted in unique, one-of-a-kind floor length curtains, but it also made my ceiling and windows look higher in the process.

First, I found some sheer curtains in a natural colour that fit the wall of large windows and glass sliding doors leading out to my patio. I installed the curtain rod a couple of inches above the window and door frames. Then I hung the curtains, and … they looked okay. I lived with them while I thought about the problem. (I find it's a good idea to step back and think about something before I rush to change it.) I wanted to give myself some time to solve this problem once instead of having to redo it several times. Then it hit me: if I moved the rod much closer to the ceiling, the ceiling and windows would appear taller and more elegant. Of course, that would mean I would either have to buy new curtains (the ones I just bought didn't meet the floor when hung from the top of the wall) or I would have to figure out a way to alter them so they were longer.

The solution: a wide hem in a coordinating fabric attached to the bottom of the existing curtain. All I needed was a few yards of scrumptious silk.

After moving the curtain rod closer to the ceiling (it's easy – I'll show you how in 'Move a Curtain Rod to Make Windows Appear Larger' on page 128), I measured the distance between the top of the hem on the drape (which would be cut off in my case because the sewing line would show if I tried taking out the hem) and the floor. The fabric was simply sewn along the bottom of the curtains. It was just a simple modification, but what an enormous difference it made in the room.

BARBARA'S BEST-KEPT SECRET

If your windows are narrow, you can give the illusion of a wider expanse by placing the track 8 to 15cm (3 to 6 in) away from the edge of the window. The curtains will look as if they are covering additional windows, and the extra fabric gives the room a luxurious, dramatic feel.

Height of Style

. . . .

MOVE A CURTAIN ROD TO MAKE WINDOWS APPEAR LARGER

Time: About 40 minutes

Here's how to adjust a curtain rod and give the illusion of larger windows.

WHAT YOU NEED

Curtain rod and hardware

Long tape measure

Spirit level

Stud finder

Power drill with screwdriver bits

Screws and wall plugs

Hammer

Pencil

Putty knife

Joint compound

Wall paint

Curtain fabric

Additional fabric (if necessary to make the curtains longer)

HOW TO GET IT DONE

1. Decide where you want to hang your curtain rod by holding the rod up to the wall. A good placement is about 50 mm (2 in) below the ceiling. However, if you have large finials, make sure they will fit without touching the ceiling. All curtain hardware should clear the ceiling by at least 25 mm (1 in).
2. Use your level to make sure the position is straight. Be sure your curtain rod will support the weight of the curtains. If the curtains are very heavy, or the curtain rod is longer than about 1.2 m (4 ft), use a centre bracket for additional support. In general, long rods come with the additional centre bracket.
3. Once you've decided on the placement of the brackets, use your pencil to lightly mark the top of the bracket and the screw holes on the chosen site.
4. Drill a hole at each mark and insert a wall plug. Then screw each bracket in place on the wall.
5. Fit the rod on its brackets and check that it is level.
6. Use a putty knife to apply joint compound to fill holes left when you removed the rod from its original, lower position. Allow the patches to dry and then repaint them with your wall colour.

Moving the curtain rod higher made my window appear taller.

7. If you are altering your original drapes, sew a fabric panel to the bottom of the drape to meet the floor. Press and hang.

Adding a band of luxurious fabric to the hems of my off-the-shelf curtains instantly gave them a custom look.

Door Prize

Doors are pretty simple – usually a rectangular panel of some kind of material that helps us access buildings and rooms and close off cupboards or other storage areas. I think doors are a neglected part of a room – people seem to forget that their surface offers opportunity for paint and other embellishments. Changing your door's colour, finish and general appearance can bring a room's décor together. Changing the door itself can represent a major upgrade to your home. For example, replacing inexpensive hollow-core doors with wood raised-panel doors can make a big difference in the appearance, desirability and value of your home. Even switching conventional brass-finish door knobs with stylish nickel-plated versions can transform your door's personality! So don't forget about your doors when embarking on a renovation or decorating project.

Exterior Doors

The front door is one of the first things people see when they come to your home. It makes a statement and sets the tone for the rest of the house. Your door should say, 'Come on in!' rather than 'Keep out!' To convey a sense of friendly warmth, a front door should be freshly painted or stained. Door handles and hardware should be polished, not tarnished. House numbers should be clearly visible from the street. Accessories such as the letterbox and doorbell should coordinate with door hardware and must be in good working order. Ample lighting is a must: one overhead light or sconces flanking the door are true beacons for homecomings.

Dustbins, bicycles, toys and other stray stuff can be relegated to the garage or a corner of the back garden. Make your front door even more welcoming with inexpensive accessories that say 'Hello' in the most charming way. Wind chimes, flowers in containers or window boxes (in winter months, an evergreen and winter-flowering plants in a large pot add life) bring kerb appeal right to your doorstep.

A brand new front door can also make the façade of your house look brand new. Most exterior wooden doors are made of solid wood using frame and panel construction to counteract the effects of climatic or seasonal changes.

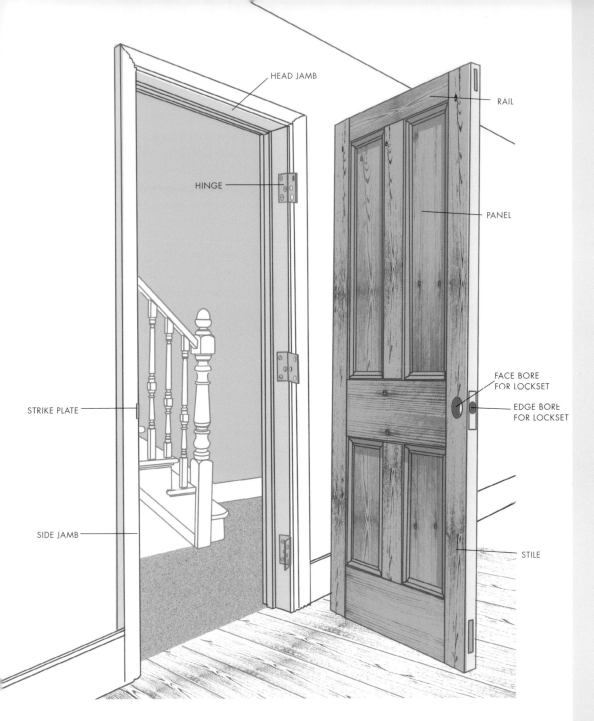

HEAD JAMB

RAIL

HINGE

PANEL

STRIKE PLATE

FACE BORE
FOR LOCKSET

EDGE BORE
FOR LOCKSET

SIDE JAMB

STILE

Wood doors can be painted or stained. If painting, consider using high-gloss paint for an elegant but easy-to-clean finish.

Steel doors have energy-efficient foam-core insulation and are fully weather stripped by the manufacturer. They resist shrinking, swelling and warping. Their tough steel construction withstands extreme weather with little maintenance. Steel doors come preprimed and ready to paint any colour you like. Many steel doors come primed with a rust-resistant finish. 'Raw' steel doors need to be primed first with a rust-resistant primer and then painted.

Glass fibre and uPVC doors offer the same energy-saving and easy installation qualities as steel doors. They sometimes have a moulded wood grain texture so they give the appearance of a real wood door when painted or stained. Yes, you can stain a plastic door! These are also highly weather-, scratch- and dent-resistant. This makes a plastic door a great choice for busy family homes in extreme climates. One caveat: glass fibre and uPVC doors (and windows) are expensive.

Interior Doors – The Inside Story

Interior doors give us privacy and, with the help of walls, define spaces in a home. We don't think a lot about our inside doors unless they're stuck or squeaking. But doors can add to the decorative statement your house makes. And while replacing interior doors is a job for serious do-it-yourselfers, you can do a lot to enhance the doors you already have (and keep them from sticking while you're at it).

Many of my friends, especially those who live in city apartments, have plain wood veneer doors. They have a tendency to look drab in their natural finish. A lick of semi-gloss paint brightens them up in no time. Picture frame moulding, mitre-cut to form corners, and applied to the door in one, two or three rectangles with glue and pins, can be painted to resemble traditional raised panel doors. These panels can be lined with a bit of padding and fabric to add richness and texture to a door. In fact, the insets of genuine panels doors can also be enhanced with fabric, leather, hessian or other materials. Decorative panels attached or set into a plain door add a hand-crafted look.

I found some beautiful carved wood panels at a junk shop. They were very inexpensive but I knew they would be elevated to artisan status when set into my plain, flat doors. It's an easy woodworking project that results in a very expensive designer look. I bought four panels for each of the four doors of my cupboard. You can try the same technique with your cupboard doors, as long as they have a solid core or solid wood framing (such as louvred cupboard doors – the centre slats can be easily cut out). If you're stuck with hollow core doors, consider placing lightweight decorative panels or wood trim to the front using wood glue, nails, or small L-brackets. Attach with wood screws and a screwdriver.

DEFINING MOMENT

HOLLOW-CORE DOORS: Hollow-core doors are made from two thin veneer plywood or hardboard faces. Interior cardboard supports help keep the door rigid. Hollow-core doors are lightweight and inexpensive, provide a smooth surface for paint or stain, and are easily installed or replaced. The cons? They're easy to damage and are ineffective as sound barriers.

MDF DOORS: Solid medium-density fibreboard (MDF) is an engineered wood product that is produced in sheets and then milled like hardwood. It is extremely dense and heavy with a flat, smooth surface that takes paint beautifully. It's highly sound-resistant, sturdy and very affordable.

SOLID-CORE DOORS: Solid-core doors are made from high-density fibreboard or hardboard. A top-quality solid-core door will also have hardwood support where screw holes are located for fixing hinges and latches. These doors, like solid wood doors, come in raised panel and flat-panel styles. They can be stained or painted.

SOLID WOOD DOORS: High-quality wood doors can be very expensive. Not only is solid hardwood expensive, but wood doors also take time to manufacture because they must be kiln- and air-dried to prevent warping or cracking. Joints must be carefully manufactured to withstand stress. However, you can find old wood doors at reclamation yards. Old doors are often well made, but because door sizes were not standardized until the middle of the 20th century and sometimes not even then, old wood doors will most likely have to be modified by a carpenter in order to fit for your openings. However, this could still be less expensive than buying brand new wood doors.

INSWING (I/S): A door that opens into a room.

OUTSWING (O/S): A door that opens out.

LEFT HAND: When you look at the door from the outside, I/S door hinges are on the left, and O/S door hinges are on the right.

RIGHT HAND: When you look at the door from the outside, I/S door hinges are on the right, and O/S door hinges are on the left.

LIGHT: This is a pane of glass in a door that lets in light.

DIVIDED LIGHT: These panes of glass are or appear to be divided.

GRILLE: This is a plastic, wooden or metal grid that is applied on top of solid glass to give a door (or window) the appearance of divided lights.

Door Redo

TRANSFORM INTERIOR SOLID-CORE DOORS WITH DECORATIVE PANELS

Time: 1 day, including painting and drying time

It's really very easy to jazz up a dull interior solid-core door. Here's how.

WHAT YOU NEED

2 sawhorses

2 lengths of stout timber

Screwdriver or power drill with screwdriver bits

Decorative panels with frame for setting into door

Pencil

Jigsaw

Power drill

L-shaped picture moulding to fit around the outside of the panel

16 small rectangular metal braces

25-mm (1-in) screws

Primer

Paint

Paintbrushes

HOW TO GET IT DONE

1. Set up the sawhorses and lay the beams across them to hold the door as you work.
2. Remove the door by unscrewing the hinges. Save all the hinge hardware so you can reinstall the door when the panels are in place.
3. Decide on the placement of your panel: I wanted mine centred. You can also place the panel slightly higher, leaving a wider area at the bottom of the door. It's completely up to you.
4. Lay the door and the panel flat on the floor and trace around the panel with a pencil.
5. Lay the door across the beams on the two sawhorses. Make sure they support the door on either side.
6. Cut out the marked area of the door with a jigsaw. Start the cut by

I stapled fabric on the back of the open panels to add colour and texture – and to hide my clothes from view.

drilling a small hole on the inside corner of the traced area and cutting down one long side of the marked area. Saw along the marked line: this will ensure adequate clearance for the decorative panel to fit in the cut-out.

7. Don't let the centre fall out because it might tear the veneer off the door. As soon as you are finished cutting the long side of the panel, slide the door over so the beam is supporting the cut side. Then cut the other long side. When that cut is finished, slide the other beam underneath. Proceed with the top and bottom cuts.

8. Remove the panel you have cut. Now you have a door with a big rectangular hole in the middle!

9. Check that the decorative panel fits into the opening. It should be slightly smaller than the opening.

10. Create a support for the decorative panel by attaching the picture frame moulding to the back of the door. Do this by screwing on six metal braces. One should be placed in each corner, and another one should be placed in the middle of each side.

11. Now it is time to paint the door, brackets and moulding. It will be difficult to paint them once the decorative panel is installed, unless you are painting that as well. In that case, you can prime and paint everything at the end. I didn't want to paint my panels, however.

12. Allow the primer and paint to dry completely (about 3 hours).

13. Now you can install the panel. Drop the panel into the opening you made. It should fit snugly on the ledge you created with the moulding.

14. Attach the panel with the four remaining metal braces, fitting one in the middle of each side. Attach them on the same side as the other braces you installed earlier. Touch up the braces with a bit of paint.

15. Reinstall the door.

My finished closet doors are one of a kind, and I 'made' them myself!

That's the Rub

FIX A DOOR THAT'S RUBBING
Time: About 20 minutes

A rubbing door does not have to be an annoying fact of life. This quick fix will get rid of rubs forever.

WHAT YOU NEED
Screwdriver
Toothpick
Hammer
Finish nail
Nail set (if you need to touch up the door frame)
Wood filler (if you need to touch up the door frame)
Paint (if you need to touch up the door frame)

HOW TO GET IT DONE
1. Check and tighten all hinge screws to determine where the door is rubbing (top, middle or bottom). If it is rubbing on top, loosen the top hinge screws about halfway (do not remove). If it is rubbing on the bottom, do this to the bottom hinge. Take a toothpick and slide it behind the hinge on the side toward the centre of the doorjamb and tighten the screws.
2. If the door is still rubbing, locate the area of damaged paint on the doorframe. Take your hammer and finish nail and nail into the wood between the doorstop and frame edge until the nail is set.
3. If you are planning on retouching the doorframe after you have adjusted the door, make sure to use a nail set to sink the nail below the surface of the wood. Fill in the shallow hole with wood filler for a completely smooth surface for your paint touch-up.

Door Magic

OPEN A LOCKED BATHROOM OR WC DOOR

Time: 1 minute

Once not too long ago, a friend of Zach's locked himself in our bathroom. He panicked, but I didn't. I had him out in a minute, without damaging my door. I wiped away his tears, gave him some milk and cookies and all was right with the world.

WHAT YOU NEED

Flat-tip screwdriver

HOW TO GET IT DONE

Most bathroom and WC doors are fitted with a lockable latch. A knob on the inside allows the user to lock the door by turning the knob through 90 degrees. The lock spindle also has a peg on the outside with a slot in it. In an emergency, simply use a flat-tip screwdriver to turn the peg through 90 degrees and release the lock.

Safe House

INSTALL A DOOR CHAIN
Time: About 30 minutes

A surface-mounted door chain, which can be purchased at your DIY store, is a simple way to make your home even safer by providing an extra layer of protection against intruders.

WHAT YOU NEED
Door chain
Pencil
Utility knife
Bradawl
Screwdriver

HOW TO GET IT DONE
1. Position the chain on the door at a convenient height. A good place to put it is just above the existing lock. Place the part that receives the chain or bolt on the door frame and trace its outer edges in pencil. Use your utility knife to cut away the door trim until you reach the doorframe. Replace the receiving piece and mark the screw hole with a pencil.
2. Use your bradawl to make pilot holes for the screws. Align the lock with the pilot holes and use your screwdriver to place and tighten all the screws (never overtighten or you will run the risk of stripping the screws).
3. Close the door and hold the keeper against the face of the door. Check that the chain can be engaged in it, and mark its screw hole positions on the door. Screw the keeper to the door.

Lock Appeal

. . . .

REPLACING A MORTISE LOCK

Time: About 2 hours for a new lock, 1 hour for a replacement

If you have moved into a new home, it is a sensible precaution to change all the external door locks, since you will never know who has keys to the existing ones. And if you do not have a mortise lock on your front door at present, you can improve its security immeasurably by installing one to work in conjunction with the surface-mounted cylinder lock that is probably there already.

Mortise locks get their strength from being set into a slot (called a mortise) cut in the edge of the door. If you are changing an existing lock, you will be able to use the existing mortise (although you may have to alter or enlarge it slightly to take the new lock). If you are fitting a new lock, you will have to create a mortise for it, and also form a keyhole through the door and a recess in the frame for the lock keeper. Install the new lock about 600 mm (2 ft) below the level of the existing cylinder lock.

When you are choosing a new mortise lock, choose one that has at least five and preferably seven levers – this gives maximum thief resistance. If you are replacing an existing lock, remove it from the door and take it with you to your local lock supplier so you can if possible select a matching replacement. This will minimize any difficulties you might have in fitting it.

WHAT YOU NEED

TO REPLACE AN EXISTING LOCK:
Screwdrivers
Pliers
Wood chisels and mallet
Power drill and twist drill bits

HOW TO GET IT DONE

1. Remove the screws securing the lock faceplate to the door edge. Then operate the lock and grip the projecting lock bolt with pliers so you can pull the lock body out of its mortise.
2. If the new lock is an exact match for the old one, push it into the mortise and check that the faceplate fits flush within the shallow recess in the door edge. Next, insert the key to check that the existing keyhole lines up with the one in the lock. If everything matches, screw the new lock faceplate to the door edge to secure it.
3. If the lock is not a perfect match, you may have to enlarge the shallow recess in the door edge or alter the height of the mortise – both jobs for your chisels and mallet. You may also have to form new keyholes in the door (see below) and fill the old ones. Then simply fit the new lock as described above.
4. Remove the screws securing the old lock keeper to the door frame. Fit the new keeper in its place (see below again). You may first have to chisel out a larger recess for it in the door frame. Close the door and operate the lock to check that the bolt engages properly in the keeper.

WHAT YOU NEED

TO FIT A NEW LOCK:

As for replacing an existing lock plus

Pencil

Tape measure

19-mm ($\frac{3}{4}$-in) flat wood bit

Coloured tape

Bradawl

Padsaw or keyhole saw

HOW TO GET IT DONE

1. Hold the new lock against the door edge and mark the height of the lock body on it. Draw a pencil line down the centre of the door edge between the two marks. Fit a 19-mm ($\frac{3}{4}$-in) flat wood bit in your drill, and wrap some coloured tape round it to indicate the depth to which you need to drill to match the depth of the lock body.

2. Drill several holes in the door edge, working down the pencil line and overlapping the holes slightly. Drill the holes about 3 mm ($\frac{1}{8}$ in) deeper than the tape indicates.

3. Use a chisel and mallet to cut away the waste wood around the drill holes and create a neat rectangular slot. Test the fit of the lock in the mortise, and enlarge it slightly if necessary so the lock slides in (and out) easily. To make it easier to pull a tight-fitting lock out, use the key to shoot the lock bolt out before inserting the lock so you can grip it with pliers.

4. When the lock fits comfortably, slide it right in and draw lines on the door edge round its faceplate. Remove the lock again and chisel out a shallow recess for its faceplate. Take care not to overshoot and damage the door edge.

5. Position the lock against one face of the door. Make sure you are holding it with its faceplate flush with the door edge and in line with the recess you chiselled out in Step 4. Use a bradawl to mark the position of the round part of the keyhole on the door face. Repeat the operation on the other face of the door.

6. At each bradawl mark, drill a 10 mm ($\frac{3}{8}$ in) diameter hole through the door and into the mortise. Then use a padsaw to cut the keyhole slots below each hole, and chop out the waste with a narrow chisel.

7. Slot the lock body into the door and check that the key fits cleanly in both the keyholes and operates the bolt smoothly. Use your bradawl to make pilot holes for the fixing screws in the door edge, and screw the faceplate to the door. Fit a keyhole cover inside and out.

8. Fit the keeper to the door frame to complete the job. Turn the key to operate the lock, push the door to and hold the keeper against the frame so the bolt is in line with the box into which it fits. Mark the box position on the edge of the frame, then transfer the marks to the inner face of the frame and chisel out the slot for the box. Fit the keeper in the slot and mark round its faceplate, then chisel out a shallow recess for it and screw the keeper to the frame. Close the door and turn the key to check that the lock operates smoothly. Job done!

Mortise locks are simple but effective devices and are relatively easy to replace or install.

Slide into Style

INSTALL SLIDING WARDROBE DOORS
Time: About 40 minutes

New wardrobe doors are a quick and easy way to give a tired room a fresh new look. If you're dealing with a very wide opening, look for sliding doors that have their wheels on the track that is attached to the floor and use the upper track as a guide only. Otherwise, simply measure your old doors and take the measurements with you to your local supplier. Consider the room in which you will be using the doors and select a style that suits your décor.

Many sliding wardrobe doors can be removed by pulling them up, out and off the upper track.

Decide whether you want finished or unfinished doors and if you choose unfinished, apply paint or stain before hanging the doors.

WHAT YOU NEED

Power drill with screwdriver bits, or screwdriver
Sliding wardrobe doors with track hardware
Long tape measure
Hacksaw (if needed to cut the new track)
Hammer
Nail

HOW TO GET IT DONE

1. Lift the old doors up and out of the track. Most ride in the overhead track: some have a small lever that you hold down to release them from the track, while others have cut-outs along the track where the rollers can be lifted free. Use your power drill or screwdriver to remove the screws holding the overhead track in place. You will not need to save any of the old hardware. Remove the bottom brackets.

2. Measure the new track hardware against the old for length. Use your hacksaw to cut the new track, if necessary. Install the upper track. If you are using the old screw holes for the new track, go ahead and install the screws. (It's helpful to have a friend hold it in position while you do this.) If the new track has a different placement, use your drill, or a hammer and nail, to position pilot holes to guide the new screws in. Be sure the screws are well seated, so the heads don't interfere with the movement of the door, but don't overtighten them because this can warp the track.

3. Place the bottom track on the floor and hang first the back, then the front sliding door. Let the doors hang to find the centre for the bottom track, then remove the doors. Mark the position of the lower track, then mark each screw hole along the floor. Attach the lower track and then rehang the doors – again starting with the back door. Attach the doors to the lower track and slide them gently back and forth. Enjoy the silent glide of your new doors.

Now that your doors and windows look beautiful and are operating smoothly (and you did it yourself!), let's tackle some plumbing problems.

Plumbing the Depths

It's a fact: plumbing problems always seem to stop us in our tracks. It's probably because we can't see a lot of what plumbing really is. Water and waste pipes are generally buried behind walls or under floors, and so what we can't see, we often don't understand. Many of us (men included) are a little scared of what goes on inside those pipes. But you don't have to be scared because plumbing isn't as intimidating as it seems. Once I understood what plumbing was all about, I found that it wasn't a big deal. It's quite logical, in fact. Once you get a grip on the basics, you'll be able to make many repairs in your house that would otherwise cost you an arm and a leg!

Why not do it yourself? You'll feel fantastic about getting rid of that irritating drip, that annoying overflowing WC cistern and the constantly clogged kitchen drain.

Of all home improvement projects, the feeling of accomplishment and pride you will get from having successfully solved a plumbing problem will make you feel like a superhero. Indeed, you will be a megastar in the eyes of your family and friends! And it doesn't have to stop with quick drain fixes and repairing basic WC trouble. You can actually update and add value to your home by learning the skills in this chapter and then combining them with many other how-to projects in this book. For example, I love the idea that you can fix and upgrade your bathroom and make it go from boring to spa-like in just a weekend or two. I want you to have the best bathroom on your street, and I want you to do a lot of it yourself.

So grab your wrench and come along with me. You don't even have to change your shoes. (I do my plumbing in high heels!)

SAFETY NOTES

Remember always to follow the manufacturer's instructions when using any product or tool, even if you've used it in the past. Follow manufacturer's recommended safety precautions when working with plumbing products. Always work in a clear area. Go slowly and always have a bucket and rag nearby to catch leaks and draining water. A wet-and-dry vacuum cleaner really comes in handy when dealing with plumbing projects: it sucks up both solid debris and water. When working with new fixtures, such as a tap or showerhead, remember to use a cloth or rag under the pliers so that you don't scratch the fittings.

That Sinking Feeling

Is there anything more irritating than a dripping tap or a basin that won't drain properly? What about those corroded 1970s fixtures staring you in the face every morning? That's not the best way to wake up! We have so much to do during the day that we should all be able to start the day as peacefully and beautifully as possible. It doesn't matter if you love to luxuriate in the bathroom or you prefer to be in and out in a matter of minutes. Having a basin and tap that work well helps you get the right start to what will most likely be a hectic day. Even the kitchen sink plays an important part in a smoothly running day: it's no fun to prepare a quick cup of coffee or boil water for a pasta supper if the sink is acting up!

Here are some simple solutions to getting your bathroom and kitchen sinks quiet, clear and looking gorgeous!

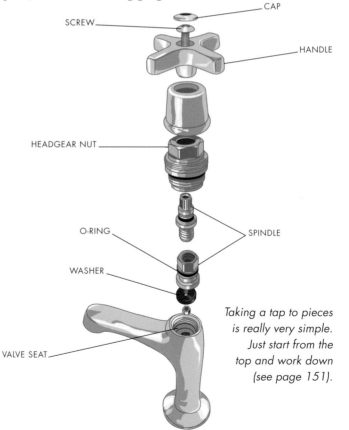

SCREW

CAP

HANDLE

HEADGEAR NUT

O-RING

SPINDLE

WASHER

VALVE SEAT

Taking a tap to pieces is really very simple. Just start from the top and work down (see page 151).

Fixing a leaky tap is a
do-it-yourself job you
can handle easily.

The Big Drip Tap Fix

REPAIR A DRIPPING TAP
Time: About 30 minutes

A dripping tap is an annoying reminder that you're wasting water and literally throwing it and possibly your hard-earned money down the drain. Old-fashioned washered taps cause most leaks. Modern taps are washerless and virtually dripless. Simply replacing an old-fashioned tap's O-ring or the washer can usually stop a drip coming from the spout or handle.

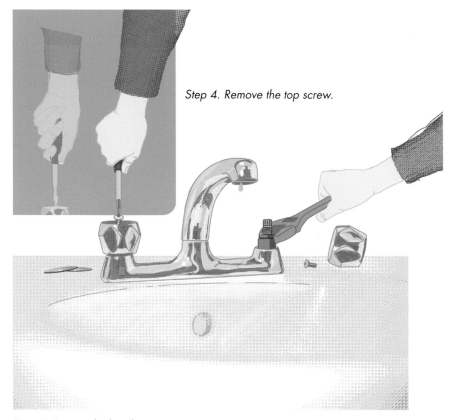

Step 4. Remove the top screw.

Step 5. Loosen the headgear nut.

WHAT YOU NEED

Plastic wrap

Towel

Flat-tip screwdriver

Phillips screwdriver

Adjustable wrench or slip joint pliers

Washer (if it needs to be replaced)

O-ring(s) (if they need to be replaced)

Utility knife

Silicone lubricant

HOW TO GET IT DONE

1. Shut off the water at the local shut-off valve located under the sink. Get rid of any water left by turning the tap handle and letting the water drain out. You can also test to make sure you actually turned off the water supply this way.
2. Place a folded piece of plastic wrap over the plughole and then cover it and the basin with a towel. These two layers will protect the sink and stop any small bits from falling down the plughole.
3. If there's a cap on the handle, gently lever it off using a flat-tip screwdriver or a similar tool.
4. Next, using a Phillips screwdriver, undo the screw that holds the handle in place.
5. Using your wrench or pliers, loosen the headgear nut. Lift the headgear out of the tap body.
6. First check the washer. It's the little disc screwed to the bottom of the spindle. If it's cracked or seems brittle, replace it. Take it to the DIY store and buy a matching one for pennies.
7. Now check the O-ring. It's like a little rubber band that circles the spindle. There might be more than one. If any of them look perished or otherwise damaged, cut them off with a utility knife.
8. Replace the O-rings with matching ones from the DIY store. It's a good idea to coat the stem with a bit of silicone lubricant first. You can use the flat-tip screwdriver to help guide the O-rings into place.
9. Now reassemble the tap by reversing steps 3 to 5.
10. Remove the towel and plastic wrap and turn the shut-off valve back on.

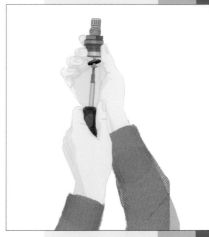

Step 6. Inspect the washer and replace it if it's damaged.

Step 7. Inspect the O-ring and replace it if it's damaged.

Plug Stopper

CLEAN AND ADJUST A POP-UP WASTE OUTLET
Time: About 30 minutes

A blocked-up sink is often caused by the stuff that collects in the pop-up waste outlet (most often hair, toothpaste, soap and dental floss). You can get rid of the buildup in just a few minutes. It's good maintenance to clean the outlet whenever you think the water is draining out of the sink more slowly than it should. Allowing buildup to accumulate month after month can cause bigger blockages that are harder to clean out. The seconds you take while using the sink will save cleaning time later on.

WHAT YOU NEED
Pliers
Rubber gloves
Old toothbrush

HOW TO GET IT DONE
1. Push down the pop-up waste lever to raise the plug.
2. Remove the plug. Clean the debris from the plug and the waste outlet with your hands (wear rubber gloves if you like) and an old toothbrush.
3. Reinstall the plug.

Take the Plunge

CLEAR A BLOCKED WASTE OUTLET

Time: About 15 minutes

I have a lot of friends who have children Zachary's age. All of us mums love doing things in the kitchen with our kids – from melting butter for microwave popcorn to making craft projects (think glue and glitter!). At one time or another each of us has faced a blocked sink, usually after an afternoon of cooking something up in the kitchen. Luckily, kitchen sink blockages can be cleared quickly.

Unblocking bathroom drains seems like a constant activity in one friend's house. She has two teenage girls with lots of hair products and makeup. And a lot of it is trying to get down the plughole. It usually doesn't make it all the way down, which is why I recommended the following technique to my friend.

WHAT YOU NEED

Rag
Plunger

HOW TO GET IT DONE

1. Remove the plug. Pop-up plugs lift out directly. If it's a kitchen sink, remove the strainer.
2. Stuff a wet rag in the overflow opening to prevent air from breaking the suction of the plunger. If you are clearing a double kitchen sink, remove the strainer and stuff a wet rag in the outlet and overflow of the other sink.
3. Place the plunger cup over the drain and run enough water to cover the lip of the cup. Use the handle to move the centre of the cup up and down rapidly and forcefully without breaking the seal of the plunger lip.
4. Reinstall the plug.

Trap It

REMOVE AND CLEAN A SINK TRAP
Time: About 30 minutes

If cleaning the pop-up stopper and plunging doesn't get rid of the blockage, you may have to clean out the sink trap. That's the U-shaped pipe below the sink. Cleaning it out seems pretty daunting, especially because it requires loosening and temporarily removing the trap so it can be emptied of the buildup that is obstructing the water, but it's a straightforward fix. It's also a job that a plumber will charge a lot for, so why not learn to do yourself? With the money you save, go ahead and treat yourself to something nice. You deserve it for being such a plumbing genius.

WHAT YOU NEED
Bucket
Pliers or pipe wrench
Old toothbrush

HOW TO GET IT DONE
1. Place a bucket under the trap to catch water and waste material.
2. Loosen the slip nuts on the trap bend with pliers or a pipe wrench. Then unscrew the nuts by hand, slide them away from the connections, and carefully pull off the trap bend.
3. Dump out waste material and clean the trap with a toothbrush. Inspect the slip-nut washers for wear and replace them, if necessary.
4. Reinstall the trap and tighten the slip nuts. Don't overtighten or you could strip the nuts. Test the drain by running water. If it leaks, tighten the slip nuts another quarter-turn.

Top It Off!

REPLACE A MIXER TAP
Time: About 45 minutes

Once you've become expert at changing tap washers, you may want to treat yourself and your bathroom to a brand-new tap. A new fixture, available in any number of finishes, from shining chrome to brushed nickel, might be just the 'jewellery' your bathroom or kitchen needs. Sometimes just changing this fixture is enough to update a drab bathroom or kitchen. Plus, replacing an old tap with a new 'washerless' model will eliminate drips and leaks for good.

Consider this: a new tap, some fresh paint on the walls and cabinets, a new shower curtain and luxurious coordinating towels are easy but effective ways to upgrade and modernize your bathroom, without spending a vast amount of money on a serious renovation.

WHAT YOU NEED
   Adjustable wrench or slip joint pliers
   Towel
   Penetrating oil lubricant
   50–50 solution of vinegar and water
   Scouring pad
   Clean rags
   Plumber's putty or silicone caulk (if your new tap does not have
      a rubber or plastic gasket for the base)
   New tap set

HOW TO GET IT DONE
1. Turn off the two shut-off valves under the tap you're replacing. Then open the tap and allow it to drain and release any pressure.
2. Disconnect the water supply pipes from the two tap tails.
3. Line the sink with a towel to protect it.
4. Remove the old tap. It's held in place by backnuts located underneath the sink, so you're going to have to go down under the sink to loosen the nuts with pliers or a wrench. If it's a very old fixture and the nuts are

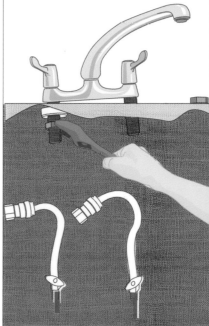

Step 4. Detach the tap from the sink.

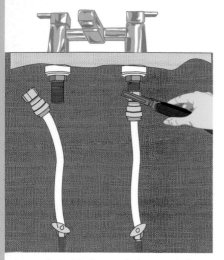

Step 10. Reattach the supply lines under the sink.

rusted or corroded, apply penetrating oil lubricant and allow it to sit and work according to the manufacturer's instructions before trying to remove the nuts.

5. Once the tap has been removed, you'll most likely see a lot of scale in the area where it was attached. Clean it off before installing the new tap. A 50–50 solution of vinegar and water will help dissolve the scale. Work it in with a scouring pad, rinse and dry off the area with a clean rag.

6. If your new tap does not have a rubber or plastic gasket for the base, you can go ahead and install it, but you will need to run a bead of plumber's putty or silicone caulk around the tap base first.

7. Put the new tap in place, pressing against the gasket or putty to assure a good seal.

8. Get back under the sink and reconnect the supply pipes. Tighten the nuts by hand.

9. Align the tap with the back of the sink and tighten the backnuts with pliers or a wrench. If necessary, use another clean rag to wipe away excess putty from around the base of the tap.

10. Tighten up the supply pipe nuts. If you are replacing a tap that comes with a sprayer, don't turn the water back on until you install that.

11. Run a bead of plumber's putty to the base of the sprayer holder, if it does not come with a rubber or plastic gasket. Insert the holder into the hole and tighten it in place with the mounting nut. Wipe away any excess plumber's putty from around the base of the holder.

12. Insert the supply tube of the sprayer through the holder from the top. The sprayer will sit in place in the holder.

13. Get back under the sink and screw the sprayer supply hose to the hose nipple on the bottom of the tap. Tighten the nut with a wrench or slip-joint pliers.

14. Turn on the water supply and test the tap and sprayer.

Note: If your tap comes with a pop-up waste assembly, follow the step-by-step instructions included with your tap kit to install it.

Feeling Flush

Have you ever flushed the WC, expecting the water to run away as usual, and watched with horror as the water level rises … and rises until it overflows? It's one of the worst plumbing disasters you can imagine happening in your home. But it's not the only thing that can go wrong with your WC. The flush handle may just go round and round when you operate it, the toilet seat may come away in your hand, or the overflow pipe may drip continuously and soak the patio below.

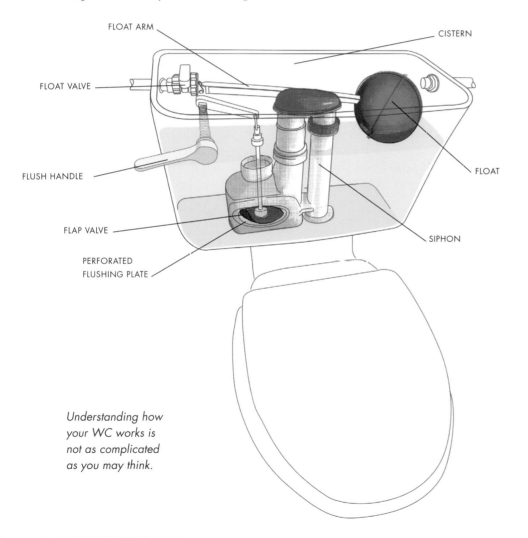

FLOAT ARM

CISTERN

FLOAT VALVE

FLUSH HANDLE

FLOAT

FLAP VALVE

SIPHON

PERFORATED
FLUSHING PLATE

*Understanding how
your WC works is
not as complicated
as you may think.*

Understanding what happens when you flush the WC may help to demystify what you need to do next time something goes wrong. It's actually quite simple. When you press the flush handle or button, a wire linkage on the lever arm in the cistern lifts the perforated flushing plate and its flexible flap valve inside the siphon. This acts as a piston, pushing water over the top of the siphon's inverted U-bend and starting the siphonic action. When you let go of the lever, the flushing plate drops down again, but the flap valve on top of it lifts, allowing water to carry on flowing up through the siphon and into the WC pan. This flow continues until the water level inside the cistern drops below the open lower end of the siphon and air is admitted, breaking the siphonic flow. The flush is over. At the same time, the float-operated valve on the cistern's inlet pipe opens, refilling the cistern with water ready for the next flush.

When the flush water enters the WC pan, the water level rises enough to start flowing out through the U-shaped trap beneath the pan. This overflow carries the contents of the pan into the soil pipe and away to the drains. The last part of the flush refills the trap with clean water and prevents drain smells from entering the room. In everyday use, the flush will carry away the contents of the pan easily, but if the pan gets choked in some way, the result is a blocked outlet. However, don't despair: you can usually fix the problem with a few simple tricks and tools.

DEFINING MOMENT

FLAP VALVE: This flexible plastic diaphragm rests on top of the flushing plate. When the plate is raised by operating the flush lever, the diaphragm is pressed against it, enabling the plate to act as a solid piston. As the plate drops down again after initiating the flush action, the diaphragm flaps upwards, allowing water to continue to flow up through the flushing plate and into the siphon. A torn flap valve can make the WC impossible to flush.

FLOAT-OPERATED VALVE: This valve is mounted near the top of the cistern and is connected to the water inlet pipe. It refills the cistern automatically every time the WC is flushed. As the water level in the cistern falls, the float arm drops and opens the valve to admit more water. When the water level is restored, the arm rises and closes the valve again. A faulty valve can prevent the cistern from refilling, or may cause it to overflow.

FLUSH HANDLE: This is the lever or button that you depress to flush the WC.

Handle It!

ADJUST A WC HANDLE
Time: About 15 minutes

A WC handle can become disconnected from the siphon lift rod so that one day it just doesn't function at all. It's the easiest plumbing fix in the book.

WHAT YOU NEED
  Wire link
  Long nose pliers

HOW TO GET IT DONE
1. Remove the cistern cover and look for the C-shaped wire link that connects the flush lever to the top of the siphon lift rod. If it has become disconnected, reconnect it and squeeze the loop up with your pliers.

Toilet Overboard!

CLEAR A BLOCKED TOILET

Time: About 20 minutes

There are few household problems as scary as an overflowing toilet. The first time I experienced this 'event', I thought I would cry. There's a real feeling of helplessness when water starts pouring out over the rim of the toilet bowl all over the floor. Don't panic! There is a way to stop the overflow, which is generally caused by a blockage in the WC trap.

WHAT YOU NEED

Flanged plunger
Bucket of water
WC auger
Wet-and-dry vacuum cleaner or bucket and mops

HOW TO GET IT DONE

1. Place the cup of the flanged plunger over the outlet and plunge up and down rapidly while maintaining a seal around the lip of the cup.
2. Slowly pour a bucket of water into the bowl to clear the drain. Repeat plunging, if necessary.
3. If that doesn't work, an object may be obstructing the outlet. A WC auger will help. Push the auger cable into the trap. Crank the auger handle in a clockwise direction to break up the obstructions. Continue to crank as you retrieve the cable and pull the obstruction out of the trap.
4. You may have quite a mess to clean up. That's where the vacuum cleaner or bucket and mops will come in handy.
5. If more than one WC in your home is backing up, the point where the waste pipes come together could be blocked. Long augers are available for these situations and are best used by a plumber. Here's what the plumber will do: if the main drain line doesn't have a clean-out access, a long auger, or 'snake', can be inserted directly through the WC branch pipe. This may require temporarily removing the WC.

Run Away

. . . .

REPAIR AN OVERFLOWING WC CISTERN

Time: About 20 minutes

An overflowing cistern is a nuisance and a waste of water. Fortunately, it's also a home repair problem that can be solved quickly. Stopping the water from running is simply a matter of finding and fixing the cause.

WHAT YOU NEED

New float
6-in-1 interchangeable screwdriver
Toilet repair kit

HOW TO GET IT DONE

1. Remove the lid and lift the float arm up. If this stops the water from running in, try bending the arm down so the float ball sits lower in the cistern.
2. If the float ball is not floating on top of the water, unscrew the old one and replace it with a new one.
3. If the toilet continues to run, there may be buildup or some kind of sediment that is not allowing the float valve to close properly. Check the flush valve and the flush valve seat to see whether there is any damage. The valve must be replaced if it is worn.

A New Seat for the Throne

REPLACE A TOILET SEAT
Time: Less than 30 minutes

As I said earlier, a beautiful new tap and some snazzy bathroom accessories can help create a spa-like atmosphere in any bathroom. Another simple fix – changing a toilet seat – completes your new look for very little money and effort. And sometimes a change of seat is all that's necessary to make a toilet look new.

Toilet seats are made in two standard shapes, rounded and elongated, and they are not interchangeable. You can tell by looking carefully at the old one but, to be sure, take it with you to the store and match it up.

WHAT YOU NEED
Spanner
Flat-tip screwdriver
Rags
New toilet seat

HOW TO GET IT DONE
1. Remove the old seat by undoing the mounting-bolt-and-nut assemblies. Old-fashioned seats may have to be removed by reaching under the back of the bowl and using a small spanner on the nuts. On modern seats (post 1960), the bolts are separate from the hinge. They are inserted through housings at each end of the hinge. Use a flat-tip screwdriver to lever the two covers open. Unscrew the bolts and lift the old seat off.
2. Most new seats will come with two square washers. If your seat came with those pieces, turn the new seat upside down, peel the protective paper off each washer and centre them on the bottom of each bolt-head housing.
3. Turn the seat over, line up the holes and bolt it to the bowl. With old-style seats, set washers on the bolts and run the nuts up snug, but not too tight. With new-style seats, start the nut on each bolt by reaching underneath. You should then be able to hand-tighten each bolt without holding the nut because they are usually self-holding. Close the housing covers and you're done!

Shower Power

A brisk shower is sometimes all I need to get me going – that and a big hug from Zach. I love taking long, hot showers after a tough day at work or on the weekends. A strong rush of water running down my back is so invigorating. Don't get me wrong, a long soak in the tub is wonderful, but a great shower is one of the few ways I can get energized and relaxed at the same time.

Are you renovating your bathroom or making decisions about a new house and one of the bathrooms is too small for a bath? Don't be disappointed. There are so many fashionable choices in showers today that a bath-free bathroom can be as luxurious and beautiful as any spa! In my bathroom, I chose a porcelain shower basin and beautiful etched glass for the door and surround. You don't have to settle for plain glass. Myriad choices in glass today make it possible to create a truly unique shower, and most decorative glass doesn't cost any more than standard glass.

I also chose a balance pressure valve for its expensive look (but not a high price tag). A balance pressure valve is made to look like an expensive thermostatic valve. A thermostatic valve is much more expensive because it gives both temperature control, as well as pressure/volume control, by using separate shut-off valves from the thermostat. But a standard balance pressure valve exerts full water pressure with just hot and cold temperature regulation. You cannot control the volume or pressure of the water coming out. But manufacturers are making balance pressure valves that look like their expensive counterparts but cost a lot less. A thermostatic valve is a luxury item and not necessary to take a great shower. But if you can get the look for less, why not do it?

Off with Its Head!

REPLACE A SHOWERHEAD
Time: About 20 minutes

It's easy to make an old shower look new. Along with changing an old tap and replacing a toilet seat, a new showerhead can perk up an old bathroom and even improve the strength of the shower flow. Why? Sometimes an old showerhead can get clogged or corroded and that can reduce the flow of water through it. Besides, a bright new showerhead is such an effortless way to transform your bathroom, especially if you want to add a massage feature. Make sure your shower floor is dry before starting this project to ensure that you don't slip. Wear trainers or other flat rubber-soled shoes. No heels here!

WHAT YOU NEED
Slip joint pliers
PTFE sealing tape
Cloth rag
New showerhead

HOW TO GET IT DONE
1. Using the pliers, twist off the old showerhead (anticlockwise), while holding the shower pipe stem.
2. Wrap the PTFE tape two or three times around the threads at the end of the pipe stem.
3. Using a cloth under the pliers to protect the new showerhead fitting, screw on the new showerhead (clockwise) until tight. Stand back, turn on the water and test for leaks. You've earned that hot, steamy shower – you installed it yourself!

No Strain Drain

HOW TO CLEAR A SHOWER WASTE OUTLET
Time: About 15 minutes

Keep in mind that a shower drain can block up just like a sink drain. If the water seems to be running out slowly after you shower, check to make sure the outlet is clear. Hair and bits of soap are the biggest culprits, making clearing the drain a straightforward production.

WHAT YOU NEED
Flat-tip screwdriver
Flashlight
Stiff wire
Plunger
Hand auger

HOW TO GET IT DONE
1. Check for blockages. Using a flat-tip screwdriver, remove the strainer cover on the outlet. With a flashlight, look for hair in the drain opening. Bend a hook end on a stiff wire and use it to pull hair and other obstructions from the drain.
2. Use a plunger to clear a blockage. Place the rubber cup over the drain and run enough water into the shower tray to cover the lip of the cup. Work the handle up and down forcefully without breaking the seal of the lip.
3. More stubborn blockages can be cleared with a hand auger. Do not confuse a hand auger with a WC auger. They are not interchangeable.

I hope this chapter has proved to you that many plumbing issues can be addressed easily and simply. A little confidence and the right tools are really all you need. Next time there's a blockage or a drip, promise me you'll tackle it on your own. In the meantime, let's get going on all small repairs and improvements you can make that will make your house and your life hum a happier tune.

Smooth Operation: Fast Fixes, Everyday Upgrades and Clutter Control

When the things around me work, my life works. Staying on top of the details – making small improvements or minor repairs, doing regular maintenance and controlling clutter – all add up to one thing: stress-free living. As I said in the beginning of this book, doorknobs that turn properly and kitchen knobs that don't fall off when you pull them make life a lot more pleasant. I almost don't go through a day without picking up a hammer or a screwdriver and doing something big or small, whether it's tightening the hinges on a door, hanging a basketball hoop for Zachary, or transforming a hall cupboard into a new place to organize out-of-season clothes. Doing all these little things around the house is like second nature to me because I've learned that maintaining my environment makes my life better, easier and more enjoyable. And I find that when I've made a small repair or completed a household improvement project, I feel as though a weight has been lifted off my shoulders. I think you know what I mean: it's one less thing to worry about, and it's one more thing to feel good about.

Many maintenance and repair jobs can be done in just a few minutes and transforming improvements can be accomplished in an hour or two, or in a weekend. That's a very small investment of time, and the payoff is huge.

SAFETY NOTES

Remember to always follow the manufacturer's instructions when using any product or tool, even if you've used it in the past. Manufacturers take a lot of time to write user-friendly instructions, and they know better than anyone about how to use their particular materials or tools. Also remember when embarking on any repair project to work in an area that has been cleared of debris, or any breakable or movable objects. When you are working with saws or other power tools, wear safety glasses and gloves. Follow product instructions.

When working with paints or solvents of any kind, make sure the room is well ventilated. Wear a mask and safety glasses for protection against fumes and dust. Please dispose of solvents in a way that complies with local environmental rules.

For example, I recently changed the hardware on my kitchen cabinets. It was easy and fun, the bigger handles make the cabinets function better, and the kitchen looks like it was completely redone! You'll see for yourself in this chapter.

Clutter is another obstacle that keeps us from getting things done. If we can't find our bills, we can't pay them. If our summer clothes are out of reach, we may end up buying new ones we don't really need or even want. If the dining room is filled with sports equipment, boxes of books and discarded toys, how can we enjoy a family meal or sit quietly and write letters or do homework with our kids?

Broken furniture, drawers that stick and claustrophobic clutter equals stress, plain and simple. Disorganized rooms and cupboards, dull cabinets, plain walls and ugly furniture conspire against us to make us feel weary and uninspired. Getting organized and fixing what's broken is going to do so much for you and your family. Improving what you have and making it pretty and functional will give you and your home a new lease of life. That's what this chapter is all about: to help you see that little changes are not trivial at all, but rather, important and even monumental in the way they can make you feel.

The Big Fix

One way to ensure that you will keep up with repairs around the house is by having tools you love to use easily accessible. I keep my tool kit in the kitchen for easy access. For me, tools are accessories as important as a pair of fabulous shoes or a great-looking watch. I wouldn't be without them. In my experience, if tools are nearby, you're more prone to use them and much more likely to tackle small repair jobs when they crop up.

Problems happen in every room of the house. In this section, I'll show you how to fix and repair a variety of household problems that I find to be the most common and that friends and women in general have asked about most frequently, from chipped porcelain to broken chairs. Sharing your know-how with your friends and family will give you an even bigger boost!

I took control of my clothes by redoing my walk-in wardrobe. You'll see the end result on page 200.

The Case of the Chipped Bath

REPAIR A CHIPPED BATH
Time: About 30 minutes, plus drying time

When a friend was having some repairs carried out in her bathroom the workman accidentally dropped his pliers on the corner of my friend's newly installed enamelled bath – and whack – the force of the tool chipped its edge. What to do?

No need to rip out the bath and replace it with another new one. (What kind of a nightmare would that be?) With a steady hand and a few simple items, I helped my friend repair the chip, and before long she was enjoying a long, hot soak. You can use this simple fix to repair a chip in any enamelled or glazed bath, basin or WC. I have even filled in cracks in tiles with this technique. Mixing enamel paint with white repair compound allows you to more closely match unusual colours, too. Chipped edges can be sharp, so put on rubber gloves before you begin work on this project.

WHAT YOU NEED
Rubber gloves
Medium sandpaper or an emery board
Clean cloths
White spirit
Wooden skewer
Glass fibre repair compound
Enamel hobby paint
Ceramic tile
Single-edged razor blade
Cotton swabs
Nail polish remover

A glass fibre repair kit and some hobby paint allows you to make a virtually invisible repair.

HOW TO GET IT DONE

1. Put on rubber gloves. Sand the damaged area with medium sandpaper or an emery board until the edges of the chip are smooth. Take care not to sand any area other than the chipped portion because the sandpaper will scratch the surface.
2. Clean the chipped spot using a cloth dampened with white spirit. Wait for it to dry completely before applying the repair material.
3. Use the wooden skewer to mix the repair compound with the enamel hobby paint on a clean tile until it matches your porcelain. Add a little compound at a time. Start over again if it's not a good match.
4. Scoop a little of the compound onto a single-edged razor blade and apply it to the damaged area. Be careful with the blade! Build up the chip by starting in the centre and working out to the edges and overlapping the outline of the chip. Scrape off excess until the compound lies flush with the surface of the surrounding area.
5. After the patch dries (according to compound manufacturer's instructions), use a cotton swab saturated with nail polish remover to remove excess repair compound and blend the edges of the repair compound into the porcelain. Allow the repair to dry overnight.

Chair Fair

TIGHTEN UP CHAIR JOINTS
Time: About ½ hour

Drawers are not the only things that changes in temperature and humidity can affect. The rungs and legs of chairs can also expand and contract with the seasons. That, combined with the wear and tear of everyday use, can loosen the joints. If not dealt with, the chair will eventually fall apart. Fixing chairs has become a way of life for me because my family and friends are always visiting for meals and games, so my big dining room table and chairs see a lot of action, all year-round. Every few months I have to round up a couple of chairs and tighten them.

WHAT YOU NEED
Screwdriver
Wood glue
Toothpick
Utility knife
Sandpaper
Screws
Bungee cord

HOW TO GET IT DONE
1. Examine the chair to locate the loose areas. Turn the chair over and look at its joints, screws and pegs.
2. If you spot loose screws, tighten them up and test the chair. That may solve the problem.
3. If the hole has become enlarged so that the screw no longer fits tightly in it, remove the screw. Then put a small dab of wood glue into the hole, insert a toothpick into the glue, and snap or cut it off flush with the surface of the chair.
4. Now reinsert the screw and tighten it. The toothpick and glue combination gives the screw something to hold onto.

5. If a screw is missing, remove another one so you can match it for size. If the screw is missing because it fell out of a too-big hole, find a screw that's just slightly bigger and longer than the one you removed. The slightly larger screw can be screwed more tightly into the expanded hole.

6. If the joints are loose because a rung has become loose or detached from its hole, you can glue and screw it back in. Gently lever the chair legs apart to free the rung.

7. Scrape off all traces of the old glue with a utility knife, sand the rung and reapply wood glue to each end.

8. Apply wood glue to the holes on the chair legs.

9. Carefully put the rung back and secure it with a bungee cord to hold the legs together while the glue dries. Wipe off excess glue before it sets.

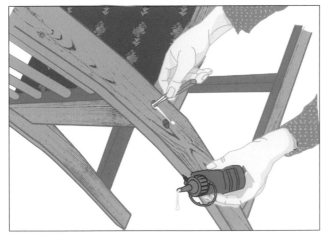

Step 3. *Put a dab of glue and a toothpick into the enlarged hole.*

Step 4. *Tighten the screw.*

Getting a Leg Up

REPAIR A BROKEN CHAIR LEG

Time: About ½ hour for repair, about 20 minutes for repainting

Weather can affect a chair, and so can enthusiastic friends and family! I had a small group over for dinner one evening, and one of my guests leaned back in my painted wooden chair and, you guessed it, the leg broke at a jagged angle. Rather than get rid of the chair, I knew I could fix it with a little wood glue and a screw.

WHAT YOU NEED

Small plastic cable tie

Power drill

Tape

Paintbrushes

Wood glue

Wood screw

Rag

Wood filler

Paint or stain to match chair

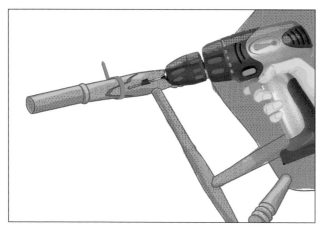

Step 3. *Predrill a pilot hole at a slight angle into the damaged area.*

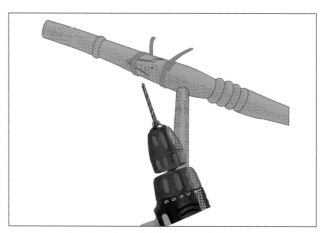

Step 4. *Go back with a slightly larger drill bit and make the very top of the pilot hole slightly bigger.*

HOW TO GET IT DONE

1. Inspect the crack and clean it out. Get rid of any loose bits and splintering wood.
2. Line up the break and secure it temporarily with a small plastic cable tie.
3. Predrill a pilot hole for a screw that will run through the damaged area without coming out the other side. Drill at a slight angle into the damaged area. Mark the drill bit with a piece of tape at about half the thickness of the leg or rung that's broken.
4. Go back in with a slightly larger drill bit and make the very top of the pilot hole slightly wider so you can countersink the screw.
5. Remove the cable tie and using a paintbrush, apply wood glue to both sides of the crack. Be careful not to force the parts apart too far or the break may get larger.
6. Drive a wood screw into the repair through the pilot hole you made to bring the crack together. Drive it slightly below the surface of the wood.
7. Wipe off any glue that comes out the sides with a rag.
8. Fix another cable tie around the repair to hold it tightly together. You can also wrap the area with tape to hold it in place.
9. Allow the glue to dry completely, overnight.
10. Cut off the cable ties or remove the tape. Fill the hole with wood filler.
11. Allow the wood filler to dry completely according to the manufacturer's instructions.
12. Repaint or stain the area. My chair was painted with a slightly distressed barn red colour. The repair is virtually invisible. What seemed like a drastic break can be repaired more easily than you think.

Step 9. Let the glue dry overnight.

Improve It

Work with what you have and develop it. That's a lesson I learned very early in life. There are opportunities all around us, and we have to keep attuned to them. This is particularly true when it comes to enhancing your home. You can make your house your own personal palace by seeing opportunities for improvement and then going with them. The goal here is to transform what you have into something better!

Dozens of basic projects will upgrade your home with ease, and none of them require special tools, professional know-how or even extraordinary artistic or design talent. They just necessitate seeing the possibilities in what is right in front of you. In this section I will show you a few improvements that I have found to be unique ways to beautify your home and give it great functionality. We'll start small, by changing the knobs on cabinets and furniture, and work our way up to building a mantelshelf for a fireplace (or even for a wall where no hearth exists).

Many of these projects can be done on a quiet afternoon (I know, not exactly a common occurrence) or a rainy Sunday or anytime when you have some time to spare. Maybe you think you don't have any time to spare, but these projects are actually worth carving out part of a busy day to do. In fact, if the only way you think you can get some of them done is by scheduling them just like a meeting or a doctor's appointment, then by all means, write 'change kitchen cabinet knobs' or 'build shelves' in your diary or electronic notebook. That way, you will be less prone to have anything interfere with your plans. Why do I think these projects – all the projects in this book actually – are so important? Because the moments you take to complete them will give you a greater quality of life that will stay with you for years to come. That's worth making time for.

Opposite: *Here I go! Getting started on changing my boring kitchen cabinet knobs.*

Before: My old, unexciting knobs.

Removing the knobs only took about 30 minutes.

Get a (New) Grip

CHANGE YOUR CABINET HANDLES

Time: About 2 hours, depending on how many cabinets you have

You'll be surprised at how fresh your kitchen, or any piece of furniture for that matter, will look with this very simple-to-do update. I did it in my kitchen, and I could not believe the difference it made.

Before you go shopping for your new handles, count the number of handles or knobs that need replacing. Remove one knob and screw to take with you when you shop for replacements. Choose replacements that are secured with the same number of screws and with new screws that are the same length and diameter as the old ones. Make sure the new knobs have a flange (the portion of the knob that rests on the surface of the wood) that is the same size or larger than the old ones. The new knobs will then cover any scratches, indentations or marks left on the face of the doors or cabinets.

If you are going from a single knob to a handle with two screws, you will have to cover up the middle hole where the original knob was with wood filler. Check out the instructions for matching stain and filling holes in 'Fix a Scratch' on page 95. If your cabinets are painted, it's even easier. Simply fill the hole with joint compound, sand down and touch up with extra paint. Because the new handle will be in front of the hole, you won't really notice the repair.

WHAT YOU NEED

Screwdriver
Slip joint pliers
New cabinet handles and screws

HOW TO GET IT DONE

1. Using a screwdriver that matches the screw head (flat-tip or Phillips), remove the old screw and knob from each door or drawer. If the screw is stripped and the screwdriver is not working to remove it, use your pliers to firmly hold the outer edge of the screw head motionless and twist the knob (anticlockwise) to remove it, taking care not to damage the cabinet.

2. Insert the new screws through the old holes and hold them tight against the back of the door or drawer with your thumb. Twist the new knob (clockwise) onto the screw until it rests against the face of the door or drawer. Then hold the knob and tighten the screw with the screwdriver.

Screw tip: When removing and retightening screws, always remember that a clockwise turn will tighten a screw and an anticlockwise turn will loosen it (righty tighty, lefty loosey).

After: *The new handles are so modern – my cabinets look brand new.*

The Great Cover-Up

PAINT CABINETS OR FURNITURE

Time: Up to 2 days, depending on the number of rooms you are doing and variables in drying time

Very often, I find that older cabinets and even antique wooden furniture are well made, but dated, dark wood finishes can sometimes give them a tired look. Even new handles or drawer pulls can't pull these pieces out of the doldrums. On the other hand, it's a shame, not to mention very costly, to replace perfectly good wooden cabinets or furniture with new versions that may not be as carefully crafted just because their finish is worn out.

Paint is a wonderful way to give new life to old cabinets, even those that aren't wood. You can also paint a laminate cabinet to give it a painted wood look or simply a fresh, updated appearance. It's amazing what a new colour will do! And older furniture can look surprisingly new when painted a chic colour, such as a high-gloss black, a soft cream or chocolaty satin brown. Painting furniture is a wonderful way to unify disparate pieces, too. A similar colour makes different styles look right together and brings out the sculptural quality of the forms.

If you want high-shine cabinets, a true gleam can only be achieved with solvent-based gloss paint. Gloss finishes are modern and sophisticated-looking. The biggest plus is that gloss paints resist grease and dirt and are very easy to wipe down and keep clean. Satin finishes are also pretty, though not as high style, and washable. So check out samples before you buy. If you use solvent-based paint, you must work in a well-ventilated room, and I recommend wearing a mask.

Replace the handles and knobs on newly repainted cabinets and furniture, and you really will have an entirely new room.

WHAT YOU NEED
Screwdriver
Plastic bag
Pencil
Warm, soapy water
Sandpaper

Power palm sander

Tack cloth

Glue

Joint compound

Wood filler

Primer (melamine primer for laminates)

Paint

Paint tray

Paint brushes in a variety of sizes

Paint thinner (to clean brushes if using solvent-based paint)

HOW TO GET IT DONE

1. If you are painting cabinets, remove all doors and keep the hinges and screws together in a plastic bag. Remove drawers. Number each door and its corresponding cabinet with a pencil.

2. Wash and dry the furniture well with warm, soapy water. Sand down any bumps or rough spots. If the cabinets and frames have a high-gloss finish, a power palm sander will make short work of creating a key on the surfaces. Primer and paint will adhere better if the cabinets are sanded smooth before proceeding. Be sure to wipe up any dust and debris with a tack cloth before painting.

3. If you are painting laminate cabinets, be sure to clean them thoroughly and remove all grease and dirt. Glue down any laminate that is lifting away from the chipboard base. If laminate is chipped, level it out with joint compound and let it dry. Sand the repair down smooth before priming with special melamine primer.

4. Fill any other large knots, gouges and gaps with wood filler. Sand smooth when dry.

5. Prime the furniture and allow it to dry completely.

6. Paint the furniture. Sand down and give items a second coat. Paint doors and drawers first and the face and any visible sides of the cabinets next.

7. When the doors and drawers are completely dry, about 24 hours, reinstall on cabinets.

Out on a Ledge

Painting cabinet doors or furniture isn't the only way to change the look of a room. There are a whole range of projects that can make a room go from insipid to inspiring, in no time. For example, if you have a fireplace but no mantelshelf, or if the mantelshelf you have isn't doing anything for your decor, it's easy to change it. I found a very unusual Indonesian shelf at a salvage yard. It already had brackets, so I did not have to add them. However, if you find something as basic as a beautiful piece of wood, even a piece of driftwood found on the beach, you can turn it into a unique, one-of-a-kind mantelshelf.

Decorative brackets and corbels (a kind of ornamental bracket that projects from the wall to support a ledge or other architectural feature) can be found everywhere, from timber yards to craft stores, so your ledge can be held up in great style. This project is so simple. Using a level will quickly and accurately assure you that an object you are hanging or installing is straight. (Simply align the level on the object you are hanging and adjust it slightly until the air bubble is centred between the indicating lines.)

Once your ledge is installed, you can really get creative. I put three beautiful framed flower photos on the ledge, taken by one of my favourite photographers. But a mantelshelf can hold all sorts of decorative and useful items: a clock, candlesticks, two or three small vases filled with fragrant flowers, family photos … the possibilities are endless. When filling your mantelshelf, keep balance and restraint in mind. You want each object to have importance, so overfilling the shelf may distract from the individual beauty of each object. The balance of texture, material and size are three more things you want to be aware of. When you are arranging your shelf, stand back and look at it once in a while and don't be afraid to edit. And remember, of course, that you can change the arrangement whenever it strikes your fancy – once a year, once a month or every week!

This exotic mantelshelf gave my fireplace a whole new personality.

A Ledge-endary Lift

INSTALL A MANTELSHELF
Time: About 50 minutes

The magic of this project is all in the material you find for your shelf. Be creative with material (reclaimed wood, brand new mahogany, knotty pine) and finishes (paint, stain, distressed, waxed) to create a totally one-of-a-kind, custom look.

WHAT YOU NEED

Beautiful piece of wood long enough to go slightly beyond the width of your fireplace
Tape measure
2 to 4 decorative wood brackets, depending on the weight of your mantelshelf
Pencil
Wall plugs (see page 24)
Safety glasses
Power drill with masonry bit and screwdriver bits
Mallet or hammer
Rag
Wood screws
Masonry screws (if applicable)
Spirit level

A mantelshelf fits together logically.

HOW TO GET IT DONE

1. Before you get started, determine what kind of wall you are dealing with. The wall around your fireplace will most likely be masonry.
2. Measure the mantelshelf and determine how many brackets you will need. Brackets should be placed 500–800 mm (20–32 in) apart. A 1-m (just over 3-ft) long board is a good, basic shelf size and should require only two brackets. Anything longer or very heavy requires three or four brackets. Determine the overhang and mark where the braces will be fixed on the wall with a pencil.
3. To fix the mantelshelf to a masonry wall, use wall plugs (see page 24) designed to hold up to 20 kg (50 lb) of weight each. The weight of both

the ledge and whatever you put on it will be carried by the strength of the fixings.

4. Put on safety glasses. Drill a hole using a masonry bit to fit the diameter and length of the wall plug. When drilling into a masonry wall, I recommend operating the power drill at a slow speed and backing it out frequently to pull out masonry debris and dust that will clog the hole and overheat the drill.

5. Insert a wall plug in the hole and tap it flush with the wall using a mallet or hammer covered with a rag to protect the surface of the wall. Repeat the process with the remaining plugs.

6. Hold the brackets in position using the marks you made earlier as a guide. Insert standard screws of the appropriate size for the plugs into the holes and tighten.

7. Place the shelf on the first bracket that has been secured to the wall. Level and align the shelf and secure the second bracket to the wall with the screws.

8. Finally, secure the brackets to the shelf.

Step 5. *Pound wall plugs in to hold brackets securely in masonry walls.*

Fire Things Up

BUILD A FIREPLACE SURROUND
Time: About 2 hours

SAFETY NOTES
Always check with your local building control department for important fire safety guidelines, especially required side and top clearance between a fireplace opening and any combustible materials. These instructions assume that your fireplace has a noncombustible surround around the immediate firebox opening.

If you love the look of your new mantelshelf and want to go a step further on your next fireplace project, consider building an entire fireplace surround. A fire surround provides a decorative frame for your fireplace and a wonderful focal point. And by the way, you don't even need a real fireplace to install one! Once you have it installed, simply paint the inside of the surround black, add some decorative tiles in front to simulate a hearth, add a couple of candles, and you've created a faux fireside in an otherwise plain room.

For this project, you can use a prepackaged kit from a DIY store or timber yard or be creative and design your own from mouldings. Have accurate measurements and make sure to have a scale sketch of your fireplace in hand when you go shopping for materials. If you are designing your own surround, buy samples of available mouldings and use wood glue to assemble short models of the sides, frieze board and mantelshelf to help you visualize the design.

WHAT YOU NEED
- Fireplace surround kit or wood mouldings
- Wall plugs
- Safety glasses
- Power drill with masonry bit
- Mallet or hammer
- Rags
- Tenon saw and mitre box (if applicable)
- Wood glue
- Nails
- Sandpaper
- Painter's tape
- Stain and polyurethane varnish or primer and paint
- Steel wool

HOW TO GET IT DONE

1. Fix the vertical side pieces first. Hold each one in position against the wall and mark the screw position through the pre-drilled holes.

2. Put on safety glasses. Drill a hole using a masonry bit to fit the particular diameter and length of the wall plug. When drilling into a masonry wall, I recommend operating the power drill at a slow speed and backing it out frequently to pull out masonry debris and dust that will clog the hole and overheat the drill.

3. Insert the plug in the hole and tap it flush with the wall using a mallet or hammer covered with a rag to protect the surface of the wall. Repeat the process with the remaining plugs.

4. If you are using mouldings to create your fire surround, use your tenon saw and mitre box to make the corner joints. Glue all joints, wiping off any excess glue with a damp cloth. Glue on the wood will prevent the stain from adhering properly.

5. Sand and clean the surface of the surround. Tape off the wall and adjoining areas with painter's tape. Apply stain, then smooth the surface with steel wool before applying at least three coats of polyurethane varnish or other protective coating. If painting, use a primer, followed by two or more coats of paint. Make sure all the products you are using are heat-resistant.

Step 1. Attach the wood surround to the wall.

Clutter Command

Clutter equals stress, plain and simple.

Messy rooms, disorganized cupboards and jumbled junk drawers add unneeded hassle to our already hectic days. I can't think when things are cluttered! So I've learned a few tricks to control the clutter. I sort and toss out the stuff I don't need or want, and I keep the necessities of life tucked away, out of sight but easily accessible.

Even small homes have space for storage. Under the bed, at the back of a cupboard, under the sink – all these spaces can be used to hold out-of-season clothes, toys, sports equipment and unsightly waste bins. That's right, even putting the kitchen bin under the sink and on a convenient roll-out trolley, instead of having it out in plain sight, reduces both visual and floor space clutter.

Donating useful but no longer needed items to charity, getting rid of unwanted junk and keeping what we do need neat, accessible and as invisible as possible mean that our personal spaces become welcoming havens instead of uninviting areas that make you want to run away. In an ideal world, every room of your house should be neat as a pin and organized alphabetically. But we know that's pretty much impossible. After all, we do have to live our lives, and making a mess is sometimes part of it. But the storage solutions in this section can help you keep your stuff restrained.

Simple shelves, for instance, are one of the most basic and useful forms of storage. Tucked into the back of a cupboard, at the end of a little used hallway, or in the corner of a child's bedroom, they provide an easy, classic clutter solution. They can hold decorative bins, boxes and baskets for all the stuff you need but don't want to look at. Or hang a curtain in front of them for complete coverage but easy access. Once you see how easy shelves are to install, you'll find all sorts of places for them.

Basic shelves are easy and inexpensive to construct using wood, plywood or MDF cut to specific lengths and widths, as is hanging them from metal shelving track (long metal strips that hold brackets) and arm brackets. For a less utilitarian look, you can attach shelves to decorative brackets. Consider saving time and skipping the cutting and sanding steps by taking your measurements to the timber yard or DIY store and having them cut the wood to your specifications.

Basic shelves can be made from a variety of materials. If the shelves are going in a cupboard or utility room, 19-mm (¾-in) plywood or pine shelves can be sanded smooth and then left as is. Plywood sheets are less costly than solid wood boards. Keep in mind that plywood does not normally come in shelf-width planks, but in large sheets, which need to be cut into shelf widths. Unless you have a circular saw and know how to use it, you will have to have plywood sheets cut into shelves at the DIY store or timber yard when you purchase the sheets. For a finished look, you can add veneer tape to the front and sides of plywood shelves. It's easy to apply with an iron because it is coated with a heat-activated adhesive.

If you are planning on making the shelves a prominent feature of a room, you can paint or stain them to match your colour and design scheme. For an expensive look, sheets of plywood veneer covered with birch, mahogany, cherry or even oak can be cut to size and coated with polyurethane for a natural finished look, stained or even painted. And, of course, you can buy hardwood boards, such as oak or mahogany, but these woods are expensive. Plywood veneer gives you the same look for a lot less. You can also buy melamine-coated chipboard shelving (usually available already cut in a variety of standard widths and lengths) if you want an easy-to-clean surface. But be aware that chipboard shelves tend to sag if heavily laden unless the brackets are closely spaced.

Shelve It!

. . . .

BUILD SIMPLE SHELVES HUNG ON METAL WALL TRACKS

Time: About 2 hours, depending on how many shelves you hung

I installed adjustable shelves in a tall cupboard in my kitchen, essentially turning it into a pantry. I store lots of soft drinks, juice, cereal and other dry goods on those shelves. And I keep Zach's favourite healthy snacks and juices on lower shelves, so they are easy for him to grab. The pantry cupboard also gives me more space in my kitchen cabinets.

WHAT YOU NEED

Stud finder (if you have partition walls)
Pencil
Tape measure
Plywood, wood or melamine-coated shelves cut to length according to size and quantity needs
Crosscut saw (or a circular saw if you have one and know how to use it)
Sandpaper or power palm sander
Metal shelving tracks (appropriate screws are included) cut to height of all shelves*
Metal brackets (twice the number of shelves you are planning on hanging)
Polyurethane varnish (optional)
Paint or stain (optional)
Spray paint (optional)
Paint brush (optional)
Power screwdriver with drill bit attachments
Wall plugs for masonry walls
Wood screws
Spirit level

* Metal shelving tracks and brackets come in a small array of colours, including plain metal, white, black and brown. If you are planning on painting or staining shelves, choose a colour that blends in best or spray paint the tracks to match the colour you are painting the shelves.

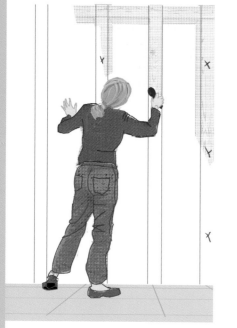

Step 1. Use a stud finder to locate wall studs.

HOW TO GET IT DONE

1. On a partition wall, locate the wall studs where you want your shelves with a stud finder and mark the spots with a pencil. To be truly secure, the tracks must be screwed into wall studs. If you have to attach the shelves between studs, use appropriate cavity anchors and make sure you do not exceed the manufacturer's recommended load limits for between-stud installation.

2. Using a tape measure, determine the width and length of the shelves you need. The length of the shelves you choose should overhang the brackets by 100 mm (4 in).

3. Cut or have shelves cut to the chosen length (and in the case of plywood, width as well).

4. If you are planning on painting, staining or varnishing the shelves, do that now to the shelves – and the metal standards and brackets, if you like. Let them dry completely before proceeding.

5. Position the metal tracks on the wall and attach them using the screws provided with or recommended by the manufacturer.

6. Attach the tracks to the wall studs with 75-mm (3-in) screws. Make sure that the slots in the tracks that hold the brackets (that hold the shelves) match up on either side of the tracks, otherwise the shelves will not hang level. Use a spirit level to make sure that the tracks are plumb so the brackets will be level.

7. Attach the brackets and place the shelves on top. The beauty of using metal shelving tracks and brackets is they allow you to add more shelves as you need them, and you can also adjust their height.

Step 7. Adjustable brackets allow you to place shelves where you want them.

Build Simple Shelves Hung on Decorative Brackets

. . . .

Time: About 2 hours, depending on how many shelves you hang

Pretty brackets turn basic shelves into something good-looking enough to show off in a living room or dining room.

WHAT YOU NEED

Stud finder (if you have partition walls)

Pencil

Tape measure

Plywood, wood or melamine-coated shelves cut to length, according to size and quantity needs

Crosscut saw (or a circular saw if you have one and know how to use it)

Polyurethane varnish (optional)

Paint or stain (optional)

Spray paint (optional)

Paint brush (optional)

Sandpaper or power palm sander

Metal, wrought iron or wood brackets

Power screwdriver with drill bit attachments

Wood screws

Spirit level

HOW TO GET IT DONE

1. On a partition wall, use a stud finder to locate the wall studs where you want your shelves and mark the spots with a pencil. To be truly secure, the brackets should be fixed to wall studs. If you have to attach the shelves between studs, use appropriate cavity anchors and make sure you do not exceed the manufacturer's recommended load limits for between-stud installation.
2. Using a tape measure, determine the width and length of the shelves you need. The length of the shelves should overhang the brackets by approximately 100 mm (4 in).

3. Cut or have shelves cut to your chosen length (and in the case of plywood, width).
4. If you are planning on painting, staining or varnishing the shelves, do that now to both the shelves and the brackets. Let them dry completely before proceeding.
5. Attach one shelf bracket to the wall for every 400 mm (16 in) of shelf span, depending on the weight of items you plan on putting on the shelves (i.e., framed photos don't carry as much weight as books do).
6. Level the shelf brackets using a spirit level.
7. Lay the shelves on top of the brackets and firmly secure the shelves to the brackets.

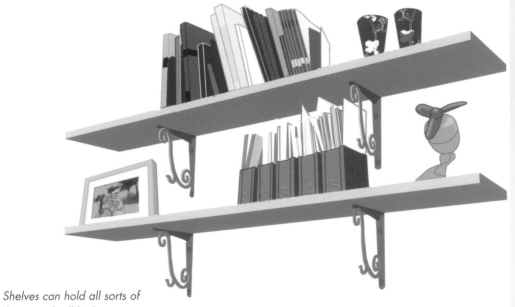

Shelves can hold all sorts of things and still look great.

Pot Luck

HANG A CEILING POT RACK
Time: About 40 minutes

My new pot rack gives my kitchen a professional look.

Storing my pots and pans in my low cabinets and drawers was not only inconvenient, but inevitably, my favourite sauté pan would end up in the far reaches of the bottom drawer, making it difficult to reach. Plus, the bulky pots took up a lot of valuable space. My solution? Hanging a pot rack from the ceiling. Not only did it free up more space, I can now see what I need and grab it easily. The most important aspect of hanging a pot rack is making sure the large bolts that go into the ceiling and hold the rack (that holds the pans) go into ceiling joists. Most ceiling rack kits are spaced to match the spacing of ceiling joists, which is usually 400 mm (16 in).

The rack you choose will come with instructions. There are different kinds of pot racks and each kind has specific installation methods. Please follow the manufacturer's instructions. Here's what you can expect if you install a hanging pot rack like mine.

WHAT YOU NEED
Ladder
Safety glasses
Stud finder
Cardboard (you can use the box the rack came in)
Hanging ceiling pot rack kit
Pencil
Painter's tape
Power drill with screwdriver bits
Wrench or pliers with rubber-coated handle

Opposite: *New cabinet pulls, a hanging pot rack...all straightforward projects that made my kitchen feel new and fresh – and ready for entertaining!*

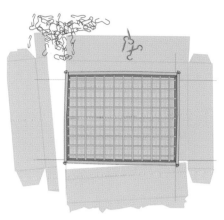

Step 3. Make a template for the pot rack using the cardboard box the kit came in.

Step 7. Hang the chains to attach the rack.

HOW TO GET IT DONE

1. Because you'll be standing on a ladder, make sure the area you are working on is clear!
2. Wear safety glasses.
3. Locate the ceiling joists, using a stud finder, and mark their position in pencil on the ceiling. Then, using the cardboard from the hanging ceiling pot rack kit, make a template using the outside of the rack as a guide. Make holes (use a pencil to poke through the cardboard) where the four ceiling hooks that come with the kit are located for attaching the rack to the ceiling.
4. Tape the template to the ceiling with painter's tape, making sure that the holes you made are placed in the middle of the marked joist positions.
5. Use a pencil to mark the four corner holes on the ceiling. This will be where you will drill.
6. Drill holes using the bit size the manufacturer recommends and then screw in the heavy eyehooks that will hold the chain of the rack. For leverage, use a rubber-coated handle of a wrench to turn the hooks. It won't mar the chrome or finish of the hook and it will save your hands!
7. Next, hang the chains that attach to the rack. It's best if the rack is placed at a height that's easy for the cook in the house to reach. Be mindful of how far your pans with long handles will hang. You may have to try a couple of chain lengths before you get it right.
8. Once everything is in place, hang your pots!

On a Roll

INSTALL A WASTE BIN TROLLEY
Time: Less than 30 minutes

Another way to clean up your kitchen and give yourself more floor space the same time is by installing a pull-out waste bin underneath your sink. Who wants to stare at a waste bin when they're eating anyway? Not me! Installing a waste bin trolley, available at most DIY stores, makes the bin even easier to access. If the bin glides out easily, children and others will be less likely to open the cabinet door and toss the waste in and miss the bin in the process. And the easy gliding action of the trolley lets you pull it out when you're cooking and toss waste into the bin easily.

The kits are easy to install with just a screwdriver! One caveat: measure the space before you buy to make sure that the trolley will not interfere with any pipes under the sink. Most kits come with the appropriate-size bin. It may be smaller than the one you are using now. I think having a smaller bin in the kitchen is a good idea. You're less likely to have a lot of rubbish in the kitchen if the bag gets filled up faster. Take it out to the dustbin, where it belongs!

WHAT YOU NEED
Pull-out waste bin kit
Pencil
Power drill with screwdriver bits

HOW TO GET IT DONE
1. Remove the bin from the trolley.
2. Place the trolley in the location under the sink.
3. Using a pencil, mark the screw holes and remove the trolley.
4. Drill pilot holes on the four marks.
5. Place the trolley assembly back, lining up the pilot holes with the holes in the trolley.
6. Screw the trolley in place. Make sure it glides easily in and out.
7. Place the bin inside, fit a bin liner and start using it!

A bin trolley keeps kitchen waste out of the way.

Wardrobe Control

My waste trolley and new pot rack completed my 'renovated' kitchen. They, along with pantry shelves, new knobs and drawer handles, were really all it needed to look neat and up-to-date. Once I saw the dramatic results in my kitchen, I wanted to make changes elsewhere. The bedroom was a logical choice for me because I have lots of clothes, shoes and accessories that need to be accessible but stored neatly away.

My walk in wardrobe was a good place to start. I had old wire shelves and poles, and they just were not working for me. It may be walk-in, but it's not especially large. Many of you probably have similar ones. After I found out how much it costs to have a professional company come in and redo just one such wardrobe in my house, I knew I had to come up with a better, less expensive way. Luckily, most DIY stores now sell all the components you need to create storage-friendly wardrobes.

Once my new wardrobe was in place and filled with the season's clothing, I still had to find a place to stow out-of-season outfits. I have a guest room with a traditional bed with loads of room underneath it. While cardboard under-the-bed storage boxes are inexpensive, they are not especially sturdy or attractive. I knew I could turn some old dresser drawers into long-lasting, customized storage units on wheels. You can use the drawers from a bureau you're getting rid of, or find them at a local secondhand furniture store. Before you start, measure the space under your bed to make sure the drawer slides easily under it – and allow for the height of the castors, which may add up to 50 mm (2 in). New handles and a coat of paint (inside and out because the drawers will be pulled out some of the time) will also make them look less like a drawer and more like a customized storage box.

Wardrobe Case

ORGANIZE A BEDROOM CUPBOARD

Time: Less than 1 day (not including shopping time!)

Redoing a walk-in wardrobe doubles its space capabilities.

Before: *My old walk-in wardrobe wasted a lot of valuable storage space.*

WHAT YOU NEED
- Screwdriver
- Joint compound
- Sandpaper
- Paint
- Paintbrush
- Tape measure
- Flat pack wardrobe organizer, shelves and rails

HOW TO GET IT DONE
1. Remove any old shelving and rails from the wardrobe. Use a screwdriver, if necessary, to remove units that are screwed to the wall.
2. Patch any holes in the walls that your 'demolition' left behind with joint compound and smooth the repair with sandpaper. (See 'Patch Small to Medium Holes in Plasterboard' on page 67 for wall-patching how-to.)
3. Apply a fresh coat of paint and allow it to dry before proceeding.
4. Measure the height, width and depth and take them to a DIY store or retailer that sells wardrobe storage systems. Choose a combination of shelving and rails that fit your needs and your wardrobe.
5. Most units will come 'flat packed' and are assembled with an Allen key, which is usually included with the kit.
6. Assemble the kit according to the manufacturer's instructions and install it in your wardrobe.

After: Assembly of my new wardrobe system was easy, and you can see what a huge difference it made – at a fraction of the cost of a custom job.

Undercover Operation

CREATE AN UNDER-THE-BED STORAGE BOX

Time: Less than 1 hour, plus drying time

The space under your bed is one big empty parking space. Fill it up with these storage 'wheels'.

WHAT YOU NEED

Old drawer
Soapy water for cleaning
Clean rags or paper towels
Fine sandpaper
Screwdriver or power drill with screwdriver bits
New handle (optional)
Wood filler (if necessary when changing handle)
Wood primer
Paintbrushes
Emulsion paint (your choice of colour)
Four plastic screw-on castors
Pencil
Enough sturdy fabric to cover the length and width of the drawer
Tape measure
Scissors
Sewing machine or fabric glue (available at any craft store)
Velcro strips

HOW TO GET IT DONE

1. Clean your drawer inside and out with mild soapy water. Dry it with clean rags or paper towels, then sand down any rough spots with fine sandpaper. Wipe away any sawdust with a barely damp paper towel.
2. Remove the handle from the drawer with a screwdriver. If you're using the existing handle, set it and the screws aside in a safe place. If you're using a new handle that doesn't match the existing holes, fill those holes with wood filler, let it dry and sand it down. If your new handles do match the existing holes, don't paint over the openings.

BARBARA'S BEST-KEPT SECRET

If you're storing woollens or other natural fabrics, cedar balls or bars, available at most department stores, are a kid-friendly, environmentally safe way to discourage moths from chomping on your favourite clothes.

3. Paint the drawer inside and out – except for the bottom – with wood primer. It will cover up knotholes, stain or finish on the drawer front and give you a clean base to start. After the primer is dry (about 1 hour), paint the drawer with your favourite colour. Let the paint dry completely before proceeding, about 2 hours.

4. Mark the castor placement: one in each corner. The wood on the bottom of your drawer should be soft enough to screw into easily. If it's not, mark the screw holes with a pencil. Put pressure on the marks with your screwdriver to make small indentations, called pilot holes, to make it easier to drive the screw in with your screwdriver.

5. Attach your castors to all four corners with a screwdriver or power drill with screwdriver bits, using the pilot holes as a guide.

Step 1. *Sand down any rough spots in the drawer to get a smooth surface for painting.*

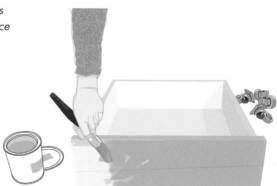

Step 3. *Prime and paint the drawer.*

6. Reattach the drawer handle. If you're using new handles, mark the screw holes, drill and attach the new handle with a screwdriver.

7. For long-term storage, it's best to protect your things with a cover. Choose a sturdy fabric, such as heavyweight canvas. You can also use denim or another heavy-duty fabric.

8. Measure the top of the drawer front to back and side to side, using the top of the sides and the back as a starting point. The goal is for the fabric to sit on top of the sides and back and just meet the front of the drawer. The drawer front is usually higher than the sides and back, and because you want the fabric to sit flat, you will attach the fabric only to the sides and back.

9. Cut a piece of fabric 25 mm (1 in) larger than the measurement all the way around.

10. Hem the fabric by turning it under by 12 mm (½ in) twice all the way around so the hemmed fabric sits on top of the sides and back rail of the drawer and just meets the front of the drawer. Sew or tack down the hem with fabric glue.

11. Attach self-stick Velcro strips right on top of the two sides and back edge of the drawer. The width of the Velcro might be slightly wider than the drawer sides. If this is the case, simply press the Velcro so it fits snugly on the sides. Take the Velcro tape off the top piece, lay the fabric on top and attach.

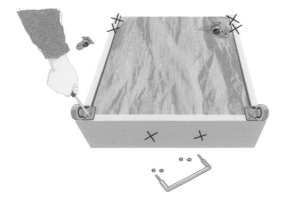

Step 5. *Screw on the castors.*

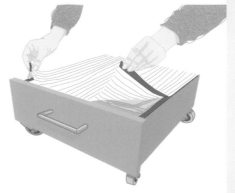

Step 11. *Attach the drawer cover with Velcro strips.*

Hallway Welcome

Organizing rooms and cupboards using some of the suggestions here will bring a new sense of order to day-to-day living. It is remarkable that simply having things in order and in a place where they can be easily located can be so good for your soul. There is one area of the house that I haven't talked about, and it's one that I think is often neglected: the hallway.

There's nothing worse than stepping into your house and being greeted with toys, assorted jackets and shoes, rubber dog toys and so on? Come on. You know exactly what I mean!

The front entrance is so important: it's the first impression you and your guests have of your home. The hallway should make the transition from the outside world to your private space a smooth and welcoming one. Keeping it neat, pretty, personal and functional is key. That way, the minute you come through the door, you can relax and the cares of the day can be left on the doorstep.

Before: *My old hallway wasn't very hospitable.*

After (opposite): *A place to sit, a mirror to do a last minute lipstick check before a big date, some lovely lighting and favourite books and keepsakes give my hallway a lot of 'Wow!' factor.*

A cushion for the stool changes the look of the hallway table.

Entry Organized

ORGANIZE A HALLWAY

Time: ½ day (or 1 day if you paint the hallway)

Here are the elements of a happy, warm and welcoming entrance to a house, and they can be used in even the smallest of hallways.

WHAT YOU NEED

Bench or small chair
Side table
Lamp
Plant(s)
Small clock
Personal items, such as special photos or mementos

HOW TO GET IT DONE

1. Clear everything out of your hallway. Use another room as a 'staging area' to sort through what you have.
2. Clean the hallway and repaint, if necessary.
3. Start going through the items that were in your hallway. Store anything that doesn't belong there (tools, toys, etc.) in an appropriate place. (How about on those shelves you built or in the under-the-bed storage boxes you made?)
4. Start adding back essential items. Consider a bench or small chair. It's both useful and beautiful. A cushion makes it the perfect place to put on or take off shoes. A side table is perfect for setting down a package. It can be a long sideboard or a tall, round candle stand. Be sure to add a small bowl for keys and a basket for mail. A lamp adds an extra source of light, brightens up a dark hall and highlights personal items displayed on the table. Plants add life – literally – to a space. Be sure to select a plant that does well in low light, such as a philodendron. A clock will be helpful so you know if you're running late! Finally, add personal touches such as a favourite picture, some sea shells that remind you of a special beach holiday, or small collections to act as happy reminders for you and serve as focal points of your life for visitors.

IT'S TIME TO VENT!

If you have warm-air central heating or a whole house air-conditioning system (lucky thing!), you may have large wall vents in every room. Great system, unattractive vents! So how can you minimize the visual impact of these utilitarian features? Cover them up, of course. Now, you cannot completely cover vents with a solid material. That will defeat their purpose (and keep you pretty cold in the winter). But you can disguise them very easily.

First, paint the vent the same colour as your wall. Most vents are metal so they need to be sanded lightly and then primed before the final coat goes on. Once you have that done, stand back and see if it's enough of a cover-up to make you happy. If not, try my trick with beaded or shell curtains. I found mine at a small home design store – but large retailers also carry them.

Because my wall vents are quite large, I bought extra shell curtains and cut up one set and tied each strand to the bottom on the ones I hung. That way they reached the floor and created a long, elegant seamless look.

In order to keep the shells from being blown around and sounding like a wind chime (the biggest wind chime in the world!), I took a clear plastic dowel and tied the bottom of the strands to it. I secured the dowel to the floor with double-stick tape. It's really that easy!

The vents are less noticeable now.

The delicate shells add a fascinating element of texture and light movement to the hallway.

Get Comfortable in a Clutter-Free Zone!

Finally, after everything is put away and you feel completely decluttered, take a moment and think about yourself. Everyone needs a comfortable, beautiful spot to call her own. Carve out a niche wherever you can find it – in a spare bedroom, a corner of your family room or even a back porch or conservatory. It's so important to have a place to retreat to when things get hectic. For me, it's just a corner of my living room, blocked off by simple sheer fabrics and a wooden panel hung from the ceiling to create another 'room' within a room.

I found an exotic daybed, and that really is all there is to my little sanctuary. I wrapped a standard twin-size mattress in a pretty length of silk and topped it with lots of soft pillows in luxurious fabrics. (Pillows are a great way to decorate; they're affordable and easy to change by whim or season.) Colourful lanterns hung from the ceiling and two plump leather ottomans give the area an exotic feel. A sturdy coffee table to hold books and a cool drink make the space practical, too. Anyone can do this, even on a smaller scale. A comfortable chair and footrest, some pillows and a comfortable throw, and a pretty reading lamp can turn any corner into a clutter-free retreat.

If a little guilt is creeping in about making a space for yourself, remember that giving yourself the gift of quiet and order is one that reverberates and reaches everyone in your life. If you take a moment for yourself to reflect in comfortable, tidy surroundings, you will be so much more ready to face the challenges of the day. Every morning, whenever I can, I sip some tea and focus my mind while sitting cross-legged in my daybed. It's a wonderful way to start my day.

Opposite: *This simple screen, found at a flea market, creates just enough privacy for my special living-room sanctuary.*

Panel Magic

CREATE A PRIVATE SPACE
Time: About 30 minutes per panel

Add a personal touch by using beads or vintage jewellery as tiebacks for your fabric panel.

Creating a private nook for my daybed was easy, and it didn't require the construction of any additional walls. I hung an antique wood panel I found at a flea market from the ceiling and flanked it with fabric panels that are sewn onto wooden rods. The clear filament makes the panel appear as if it's just floating in the room.

It's also possible to sew a pocket at the top of your fabric panel and run it on a curtain rod. Filament can be tied to each end of the rod and attached to the ceiling with cup hooks, if the rod is not too heavy Or you can attach curtain rods right to the ceiling.

I pulled back one of the fabric panels like a curtain with a simple cup hook screwed into the wall and a beaded tieback. You can make one yourself by stringing beads or even by using a vintage beaded necklace. It's totally unique jewellery created specially for your room! Hanging the panels is deceptively easy, too.

WHAT YOU NEED
Fabric or wood panels
Rods or bars to hang fabric from
Wood screws
Cup hooks
Heavy-duty clear filament or fishing line
Power screwdriver
Joint compound
Putty knife
Fine sandpaper
Ladder
Beads or old vintage beaded necklace
Fishing wire to strong beads
Cup hooks (to hold the tie back in place)

HOW TO GET IT DONE

1. Locate the position of the ceiling joist.
2. Choose where along the length of the joist you want to hang your panel.
3. I screwed cup hooks into the top of my wooden panel. Then I measured the distance between the two hooks and transferred those measurements to the ceiling.
4. Once you have made the corresponding marks in the ceiling, wrap heavy-duty clear filament around a wood screw. Make sure there's plenty of length to the filament. I actually used fishing line right off Zachary's fishing rod! You can always cut it to size later. Better to have a good length to work with.
5. Next, make pilot holes in the ceiling then install the screws with the filament attached, into the pilot holes. Drive the screws in just below the surface and let the filament hang down.
6. Fill in the indentations created by the screws with joint compound. (See 'Patch Small to Medium Holes in Plasterboard' on page 67 for instructions on filling holes.)
7. Next, tie the filament to the cup hooks on the panel to the desired height. Voilà! Instant privacy.

You've done it – your place is looking great! Everything is running smoothly, it's freshly painted and organized and the décor expresses your personality. That's a success story!

SAFETY NOTE:
Take care when working on a ladder. Make sure the area you are working on and the floor at the base of the ladder are both clear!

Epilogue

Congratulations! Now you've learned essential skills that can help improve your home. You did it yourself!

Can you see the connection between those skills and how they can help you accomplish goals you are trying to reach in other areas of your life? When we started out together, I said that making your home beautiful inevitably becomes a direct reflection of the power you have to change your life and make it what you want it to be. Spending the time working for what you really want can be hard – but worth it!

Inspiration is all around you everyday, and it is endless. From the walls to the doors and floors to the natural world and the great outdoors, your environment constantly provokes ideas. My imagination percolates each time I take on a challenge or need to find a solution to a problem at home, in my car, at the office and in my personal relationships. It takes great desire, persistence and focus to achieve success in these areas, but the result is what we all strive for: happiness and independence.

Accomplishing each project in this book will help you feel more comfortable holding and using tools. The confidence you get will in turn change your life, and the people around you will sit up and take notice. The home enhancement knowledge you now have will help expand every area of your life, whether you're a working woman or a single mum. Hey, hanging a picture frame is still empowering for me – I want every woman to feel the confidence and sense of accomplishment when she relies on herself to get something done. I truly believe that home improvement = self-improvement. It's a proven formula in my life and now, I'd like to think, in yours.

I hope *Room for Improvement* will be your companion on your own self-improvement journey. Good luck and let me know how you do! Please e-mail me at: roomforimprovement@barbarak.com.

Resources and Credits

UK Resources

Amazon
www.amazon.co.uk
You can purchase the barbara k! female-friendly tool case online from Amazon.

B&Q
www.diy.co.uk
Tel: +44 (0)845 609 6688
B&Q has superstores throughout the UK.

Designers Guild
www.designersguild.co.uk
Tel: +44(0) 20 7351 5775
Designers Guild creates interior products including wallpaper.

Fabrics and Papers
www.fabricsandpapers.com
Tel: +44 (0)1403 713028
Online suppliers of wallpaper, furnishing fabrics and more.

Focus DIY
www.focusdiy.co.uk
Tel: +44 (0)800 436 436
DIY and home improvement supplies, available both online and from shops throughout the UK.

Homebase
www.homebase.co.uk
Tel: +44 (0)845 077 8888
This home improvement chain sells everything from plumbing products to power tools and more.

IKEA
www.ikea.co.uk
Tel: See individual shop details on their website.
IKEA is a useful source of affordable shelving and storage solutions.

Jewsons
www.jewson.co.uk
Tel: See individual shop details on their website.
Jewsons stock building materials, timber and tools. They have branches throughout the UK.

Mica Hardware
www.micahardware.co.uk
Tel: +44 (0)1785 819195
Mica is a voluntary trading group of independent hardware and DIY shops throughout the UK. See their website for details of a shop in your area.

Robert Dyas
www.robertdyasdirect.co.uk
Tel: +44 (0)845 4503004
Robert Dyas stocks DIY products and homewares. They have shops throughout the UK.

Selfridges
www.selfridges.co.uk
Tel: +44 (0)8708 377 377
Selfridges stock the barbara k! tool case, which contains all the basic tools you need to get started with your home improvement projects.

Wickes
www.wickes.co.uk
Tel: +44 (0)870 6089001
This chain stocks everything you need to complete your DIY and home improvement projects. They have superstores throughout the UK.

Wilkinson
www.wilko.co.uk
Tel: +44 (0)1909 505 505
Wilkinson stock major brand and own-brand home improvement products in town-centre shops throughout the UK.

Australian Resources

Bretts Design
www.bretts.com.au
Tel: +61 (07) 3361 0537
Building supplies and designer homewares, all in one shop. Located in Brisbane.

Bunnings Warehouse
www.bunnings.com.au
Tel: See individual shop details on their website.
This chain of hardware shops has outlets throughout Australia and stocks a wide range of DIY products.

Home Hardware
www.homehardware.com.au
Tel: See individual shop details on their website.
Hardware suppliers with shops throughout Australia.

Lincraft
www.lincraft.com.au
Tel: See individual shop details on their website.
Lincraft stock supplies for making your own soft furnishings, and also offer a 'custom made' service.

Mitre 10
www.mitre10.com.au
Tel: See individual shop details on their website.
Hardware and home improvement chain, with shops throughout Australia.

Spotlight
www.spotlight.com.au
Tel: +61 1300 305 405
Spotlight stock soft home furnishings as well as fabrics and supplies for your own projects.

Credits

Thanks to the following photographers, stylists, consultants, contractors and companies for their assistance in creating the photographs in this book.

ABC Carpet & Home, All-Cald Metalcrafters LLC, American Foliage & Design Group Inc, Archipelago, Beauvais Concepts for Asha Carpets, Michelle Bergeron Designs Ltd, Mike Bernstein Paperhanging, Lewis Bloom Photographs, Lars Bolander NY, Carmen's Custom Sewing, Carpet One, Demis Gnatiuk, Golden Oldies Ltd, Hable Construction, The Home Depot Inc, InsideOut, Kohler Co, Metropolitan Design Group, R B Carpet Inc, George Ross Photographs, Loren Simons, Stencil Ease, West Elm.

Index

Page references in **bold** refer to photographs and illustrations
<u>Underscored</u> references refer to boxed text